THE LOVE OF THE GAME

The trials and tribulations of running, managing and playing in a Sunday league football team

Bradley Ambridge

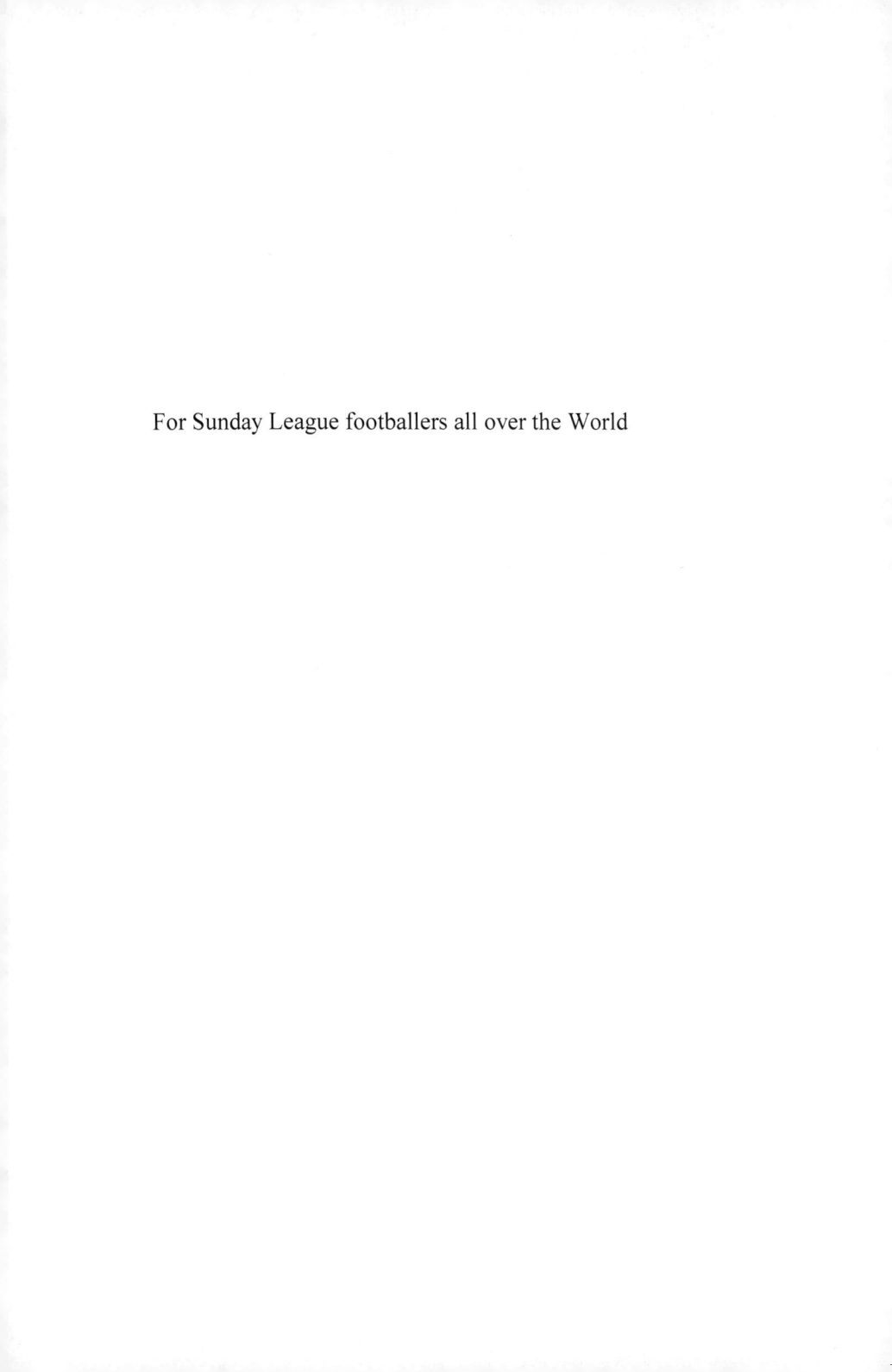

For Sunday League footballers all over the World

The team line-up on the front page of this book is as follows:

Back Row (L to R) : Adam Bunce, Abs Calim, Tony Bunce, Paul Burnham, Neil Colquhoun, Martin Hill, Huw Allanson
Front Row (L to R) : Bradley Ambridge, Matty Russell (c), Jez Mahon, Nick Sharp, Pete Sharp

Winners of the 2009/10 Sportsmanship Shield

Second Edition 2010

Chapters

1. The Ginger Hooligan — 1
2. Grass Roots — 5
3. The Richest Club In West London? — 7
4. Results & League Tables – 2002/03 & 2003/04 — 13
5. Turkish Delight — 15
6. Mind Games — 22
7. The Russian Revolution — 30
8. Don't We Know You From Somewhere? — 36
9. How Hard Can It Be? — 42
10. Results & League Tables – 2004/05 to 2008/09 — 49
11. Hyde & Seek — 54
12. Look At The Lions — 58
13. Bloody Egg-Chasers! — 62
14. What A Friendly Bunch — 67
15. London To Glasgow (And Back) — 72
16. Match Reports – 2009/10 — 75
17. And The Winner Is… — 98
18. Pretty Football Isn't Everything — 105

The Ginger Hooligan

Date : October 4th 2004
Time : 09:20am

    I am walking into an office in West London about to begin my first ever *proper* job. There is a sea of people everywhere, all at computer desks and on the telephone – it is certainly a completely different world to what I am used to. All of a sudden everybody stopped and looked round at me. As I have since found out at other jobs, the sight of a new person brings out a mixture of reactions in people; some are genuinely interested and friendly, others quite frankly couldn't careless that you have arrived… and some are ginger, but more on them later.

    At the age of 19 this was a big step for me. Whilst at school studying for my A Levels I had worked part-time at Pizza Hut and then went full-time when I realised that I had absolutely no interest in going to University - those that know me will tell you that I am not the biggest party animal around. In fact just last week I was asked by somebody what I had been up to the Saturday night before, to which a friend that has known me since the age of eight responded with "ask him what he has done this year, it will take just as long!" To be fair to him he was right – thanks Pete. Anyway I digress, if I am honest the thought of going to University genuinely scared and worried me and my mum certainly wasn't going to let me live at home for nothing. It was a case of carry on my education or get a full-time job. Who would have thought that this decision would have had such a big impact on my life?

    In case any of you were wondering, there *was* a logical reason why I turned up at 9:20am instead of the over-rated standard 9am. That logical reason was simply that I was late! And the reason that I was late was because it is notoriously difficult to park a car in West London. That's not entirely true, it is actually very easy to park a car in London as long as you either a) live on the road in question or b) don't mind having an argument with a traffic warden and getting a £120 fine. But don't panic, because if you pay that within 14 days they are kind enough to reduce it to £60. How bloody generous of them!!! Just to clarify, a) I don't and b) I didn't fancy it - after all I was already late. I had left at 6:30am that morning to make sure I was there in plenty of time. Nearly three hours to do about twenty miles – I have got a train from London to Newcastle in that time before. Before you ask why, Charlton lost three nil and Alan Shearer scored his one hundredth goal for The Magpies. The journey home seemed to take a lot longer.

My new company were a business-to-business telecommunications firm called Alternative Networks and, to be honest, the first days and weeks passed by fairly uneventfully. Everybody had been really friendly and made me feel welcome, except for one guy who seemed to keep himself to himself in the corner and, if anything, seemed quite angry and aggressive. All I could assume was that his balding, yet ginger head, had lead to a life of bitterness and abuse. As it turned out, over time we became good friends – anyone that can hold a decent football conversation usually falls into this category with me. Jez supported Brighton & Hove Albion (yes, he supports two different teams. With me supporting both West Ham and Charlton maybe that is why we got on so well) and was able to reel off story after story about the "hooligan days of his youth" which were supposedly well behind him. On first impressions, I wasn't so sure.

To give you some background information, I was born in Essex in 1984 and have been a West Ham fan from birth. My mum was a hairdresser and had previously washed both Bobby Moore and Trevor Brooking's hair – no she didn't get their autographs thinking ahead to when she would have a son and no I have never forgiven her for it. I went to my first game in 1991 against Barnsley. I can't remember the score but I'm sure that we won. Or drew. Or lost. Probably lost. It wasn't until the end of the 1990s that I acquired any real connection with Charlton. Step and Pete (more on both later) had season tickets with Ian, their Dad, but he could not get to mid-week games. It would have been rude to turn down a free ticket. It was when the North Stand was re-opened in the 2001/02 season that I got my own season ticket and spent the next three years travelling to every home and away game – hence the Newcastle anecdote before. I have had the excitement of driving on the wrong side of the road in the Peak District at 4am on a Tuesday morning after watching Charlton thrash Blackburn one-nil the night before, just to avoid some lazy sheep. A few years later at the very same Ewood Park, I had the enjoyment of watching a work friend abuse an elderly Northerner in a wheelchair, simply because he was going in the opposite direction to where she wanted to go. To be fair to her we did lose 4-1, all-but had relegation confirmed and he was trying to battle against a 10,000 strong tide of people (I say 10,000, we are talking about Blackburn here so it was probably considerably less).

Perhaps the highlight of my away trips was a weekend spent in Newcastle to watch Charlton beat Sunderland 3-1 on the opening day of the season. Darren Bent scored two on his debut and I put on a ridiculous bet with Step that 'Benty' would score more by November than Thierry Henry. Miraculously, I was correct! This however, was not the key incident. To put this into context, Step is possibly the most mellow and friendliest person you will ever come across, but whilst walking back over the Tyne Bridge after spending the evening in the exotically named Club Baha, he decided to randomly pick on two 'Geordie lasses' and enquired, with a perfect drunken slur "are you Sunderland fans?" They had no idea what to make of it, neither did we and to this day, he still denies it ever happened. Trust me, it did!

You are not to know this, but I have played in goal for most of my football career, apart from one season where I tried to give it a go on the right wing. It didn't take me long to realise that I wasn't cut out for it. I didn't have the skill or the stamina. Standing in goal definitely sounded the better of the two. Following some more football conversations with Jez, it turned out that his Sunday League side were short of a goalkeeper – how could I say no? If the whole team were like him, we would surely just scare the opposition into submission. Not only was I commuting from Dartford to Wandsworth Monday to Friday, I had now volunteered to do it on a Sunday as well – it's a bit of luck that they don't charge Road Tax by the mileage.

My adult football career was about to begin...

"Out of interest, what are the team called?" I queried.
"Knightsbridge" replied Jez in his typically unenthusiastic and dull tone.
"Knightsbridge?!?! But why do they play in Wandsworth then? That just doesn't make sense."
"Not Knightsbridge.... Nice Fridge" he said somewhat smugly, yet still in his usual voice.
"As in Happy Refrigerator?"
"Yep"

Now wasn't the time to ask any more questions. It was easier to just accept it and go with the flow.

"Oh, OK. See you Sunday!"

Grass Roots

"Sunday league football is a term used in Britain to describe those association football leagues which play on Sunday, as opposed to the more usual Saturday. These leagues tend to be lower standard amateur competitions, whose players may have less ability, or less time to devote to football, but play purely for the love of the game."
Wikipedia

I personally think that Wikipedia are being somewhat generous with the phrases "tend to be lower standard" and "may have less ability." I may only be twenty five but I have seen my fair share of Sunday league football and can confirm that the games are ALWAYS of lower standard and the players ALWAYS have less ability – in some cases less ability than the seventy-eight year old woman walking her dog around the park opposite. However, the key point here is that everybody is in the same boat. Nobody is expecting to get scouted (certainly in our league anyway) and are simply playing for 'the love of the game.'

For every young boy (and girl these days) in the United Kingdom, the dream is to grow up and play professional football for their favourite team and then go on to score the winning goal in the World Cup Final. However, for the vast majority this stays as just that – a dream. After all, over forty years worth of England International players have seen that idea quickly slip away. What chance have the youngsters got?

There are, obviously, some that are good enough to be spotted and snapped up by the Youth Academies in the area. Maybe the biggest worry of all is that over 95% of these 'talented' individuals get released before they have even had the chance to show what they are capable of. But what happens to these heart-broken youngsters? Surely they don't just turn their back on the most popular sport in the world? Of course not! There are 'special' rehabilitation venues that they can go to… the most famous being Hackney Marshes.

Hackney Marshes holds the world record for the most number of full-size football pitches in one place, and it is a fair old number. Eighty-eight to be precise! The Marshes are often referred to as "the spiritual home of Sunday league football." On a typical Sunday, over one hundred games are played at the site, meaning that roughly 2,500 players and officials all turn up for one reason and one reason only - to get involved in a football match. These numbers don't even include any spectators, although I can confirm that this really would be dependant on the weather and time of year. While Sunday League players are a hardcore, committed bunch that will play through rain, wind, sun, snow, ice, puddles, mud-baths, storms, dog poo etc, spectators on the other hand are a lot more selective. Pre-season friendlies and Cup Finals seem to be popular choices, but anything from October to April is usually out of the question.

Unfortunately I have only had the privilege of playing at Hackney Marshes once, but you will hear more about that later on in the book. For me, Sunday league football exists in the form of the West End London Amateur Football Association (WELAFA), a league that is affiliated to the Middlesex FA. Within London and Middlesex alone there are approximately one hundred and twenty five different leagues, all with an average of two divisions. Assuming that each of these divisions contains ten teams, that equates to in excess of 30,000 players that are travelling across the City just to kick a pig's bladder around for ninety minutes.

These leagues cover all walks of life, all nationalities, all religions, all races and probably even a few non-deluded Spurs fans (there has got to be some out there somewhere). One of the perks of amateur football must be the randomly named leagues and teams – the boringly named (but probably good quality) Hounslow and District Football League is soon forgotten about when you come across gems such as the quaintly named Rural Friendly League and the curiously titled North London Churches League. This is not to be mistaken with the East London Christian League, although I do have some serious questions as to whether the players in these two leagues should be doing something else on a Sunday morning? When it comes to the teams themselves, it is difficult to give anything but credit to the imagination involved in coming up with names such as The Angry Pirates, Facile Tigre (translated into English as Easy Tiger for those that are not multi-lingual) and… wait for it… Bayern Bru.

Genius!

The Richest Club In West London?

On arriving at the ground, one thing was immediately obvious – Jez was very much an exception in the team. I had expected a group of six foot-something thugs, all covered in tattoos, ready to literally pulverise the opposition into the ground. What stood in front of me were a group of pleasant-looking, polite-talking, friendly individuals, even if they were slightly older than I had imagined.

Within minutes I was being introduced to everybody. I had been nervous on the way to the changing rooms, but there had been no need. I was being involved in their conversations, included in jokes and personally handed my kit, in a similar way to how an English cricketer gets presented with his first cap on the morning of his debut. That is usually done by Nasser Hussein or Michael Atherton, but I had the honour of receiving it from the one-and-only Mr Colin Gibson. What do you mean you have never heard of him?! He is a Nice Fridge legend! I soon found out that Colin was in fact involved in law – not as a policeman, but in the industry of solicitors and such like. Amongst the other team members there was a Managing Director, two Financial Directors and another solicitor. The kind of combined salary-figures that we must be talking about here seriously could, and probably did, make us the richest club in West London. And, yes I am including Chelsea, Fulham and QPR in this! I am already referring to the team as 'us' and I hadn't even put my boots on yet – I figured that this really was the crowd to start hanging around with, even if they were significantly older than me. At the time, the average age of the team could not have been far off thirty five. Come to think of it, maybe that is why they had Jez and myself in the squad. We must have easily knocked a few years off of that!

As I put on my shiny new kit (it was new to me, but certainly wasn't brand new – it was your typical Sunday league strip!) I noticed a familiar sight. I recognised the logo on the front of the shirt. Not only was I shocked to see a sponsor's name on there, but even more surprised when it said Alternative Networks plc - the very company that I started working for just a few weeks earlier. There was no way that Jez had any direct connections with the 'powers that be' in our office, so it was either a complete coincidence or I was missing something! As it turned out, one of the previously mentioned Finance Directors was Seb White. He had been with both the club and the company for years. I then found out that he played centre back – everybody knows that a goalkeeper's best friend is a centre back, surely it worked the other way as well? Not only was I surrounded by a rich bunch of West Londoners, but one of them was effectively responsible for my salary. One good game and I could be rich. It was as close as I was ever going to come to playing professional football!

At this point I should probably mention that I asked/persuaded/dragged Step along with me to the game. I am quite a shy person until I get to know people and really didn't fancy this potentially daunting experience on my own. I seem to remember that the argument I used on Step was that there was a chance that he may get a game. I, of course, had absolutely no idea or involvement in this very vague and open-ended promise. At every possible opportunity I dropped into the conversation that he once played for Charlton Academy (that actually is true, I didn't just completely make up a fact. After all, if I was going to make something up I may as well have gone all the way and said that he was the new captain of Manchester United) but it just didn't seem to work. The poor sod spent the full 90mins behind my goal, kicking a ball aimlessly against a fence or the back of my net. At the end, in true Step-style, he said that he had enjoyed it – he is either very easily pleased or an incredibly good liar.

The game itself was fairly uneventful. Before doing research for this I was adamant that the game had finished 5-2 to us, but according to the 'official' records it was in fact 5-3. Now, this raises a number of issues. I can actually remember the two goals that I am sure I conceded, one was a header from a corner and the other was a curling effort into my top right hand corner. I genuinely have no idea about the third. Either it didn't happen and the statistics are incorrect, the shot was hit so hard that it hit the net, bounced back out to the half way line and the game kicked-off again without me knowing (unlikely, I appreciate) or I was turned round talking to Step and they simply tapped it in. You would expect to get some abuse from your team if this was the case, but they seemed so polite and friendly, they would have probably just carried on as if nothing had happened. Well, except Jez. Another point that needs clearing up is that I actually played that game and the remainder of that season with next to no vision. I now wear contact lenses every time I do anything sport related and glasses when at work, but, as I hadn't played football in so long, I hadn't had enough time to get any delivered. I queried who scored every single goal, even if it had been a Maradona-esque run from the halfway line. Fortunately we scored very few like that so I could generally just blame the sun or a goal-mouth scramble for my lack of sight. I would like to say that this is the reason that I was so poor at commanding my penalty area, but if some of my decision making in later seasons is anything to go by I think it would be somewhat harsh to blame Specsavers.

I should give you some background into the football club that is Nice Fridge. The club was formed in 1994 by Des Morris and Co (I say 'and Co' simply because I don't know their names). The obvious question here is why the hell would you call a football club Nice Fridge? And it is a question that has been asked by every single player that has every put the 'famous' kit on. The problem is that there appear to be very few people that genuinely know the answer. I am now in my seventh season with the club and the most detailed response that I have ever been given was "oh it's a long story, let's just say it was a drunken conversation one night." And this is where it gets difficult. You are not human if at this point your response is "thank you very much, that was very helpful and informative." However, if you try and dig any deeper, the conversation suddenly gets changed and by the time you realise what has happened it is too late to bring it back round again. The only reasonable thing to do here is speculate – it was either actually a very boring conversation about refrigerators and they are far too embarrassed to admit that this is how they were spending a Saturday night, or there is something a lot juicier, such as being arrested for breaking into a local Iceland and pillaging all of the frozen peas and burgers – you never know, money does funny things to people!

In terms of leadership, my earliest memory is of Des Morris himself being at the helm. He is also one of the most pleasant people you could ever meet and really doesn't look or act like a football manager. He always had a smile, always enjoyed himself and, most importantly, made sure everybody was in the same boat. Until my first game, the club had not had a genuine keeper for quite a while and he seemed to always end up 'between the sticks.' I think it is fair to say that you will not find another goalkeeper anywhere that, when conceding a soft goal, turns round to the team and says "sorry chaps."

Soon after, Des passed the responsibility onto Mr Omer Kutluoglu and this is when things started to get serious. Don't get me wrong, the club had been successful under Des and had won a number of trophies but it was always built around the founding group of players and it seemed a way for them all to keep in contact – almost like an excuse to give to the wife to get out of the house (I'd imagine that is still the reason for a number of players today). Des and Omer, along with Guy Pettigrew (Gruber) and the previously mentioned Seb White are undoubtedly the most famous players that the club has ever had. In terms of appearances, Guy Pettigrew (retired) leads the way on 190, followed by Des (retired) on 176, Seb (retired) on 167 and Omer (currently not out) on 163. For the record I am sixth on the list.

For every player and fan across the globe there is a Spiritual Home of Football. It may be Anfield for a Scouser, St James Park for a Geordie or Old Trafford if you reside in Surrey. However, as soon as you put on the Nice Fridge shirt you gain an immediate connection with South Park. Just over Wandsworth Bridge (there is a McDonalds on one side and a BP garage on the other, you really can't miss it!) and ten minutes walk from Clapham Junction there is no finer place in West London. In fact, I can only think of one place that even comes close in the whole of England but I will get to that later on. On paper, South Park is basic, very basic. There are no working showers, only one toilet, the benches in the changing rooms are falling off the walls and the pitches are notoriously bumpy and grass-less. In recent years they have moved the pitches from one part of the park to another, citing better drainage as the reason. That's all well and good but the pitches are so narrow now that you can actually jump from the touchline into the penalty area. I don't care what you think, everything I have just said sums up why everybody loves Sunday league football so much.

We do have two other 'home grounds' that are used throughout the season – probably more than South Park in fairness. The first is Hurlingham Park which is literally a stones throw round the back of South Park. Now these changing rooms are a different class all together. With a Lottery Grant on board, not only are these reasonably new, but they are always clean and tidy with private showers and toilets for each of the six rooms. There is even fully working heating which is absolute heaven after you have just been thumped five nil in the driving rain on a December morning. The venue is actually shared with the local kid's rugby club (poor parenting, if you ask me) and after every game the parents can be found in the kitchen cooking bacon sandwiches (this is good parenting, by the way) for their little ones. I don't think any of us have ever had the bottle to try and help ourselves to one, but the smell alone soon helps you forget about the game. It also makes you so hungry that the only option is to stop off at the aforementioned BP garage to get some supplies for the way home – maybe they are working together in a clever marketing ploy?!?!

Our third and final genuine home ground is Wormwood Scrubs and it is everything that you would expect it to be. The grounds are all-but shared with the famous high-secure prison and the changing rooms are in the same sort of league as South Park, although slightly larger. It is the only place where I have had the experience of playing in horizontal rain and it really isn't pleasant. At the start of any season The Scrubs' pitches are pretty good. After all, there are about fifteen to choose from. However, following any particularly wet Saturday where the ground has been churned up and the penalty areas are full of puddles, there is a mad dash to pick one of the pitches on the top of the hill in the hope that the water has drained away. Invariably it hasn't, but one day the eagerness is sure to pay off.

In terms of away games we have done our fair share of travelling. The majority of games for the whole league are actually played at Wormwood Scrubs, but we also make regular appearances at Tooting Bec, Battersea Park, Regents Park, North Acton Playing Fields and, the dreaded journey of all, Warren Farm. It is probably not too bad for most of the squad, but for us Dartfordians it is nothing short of a nightmare.

I'll leave you with a few more 'interesting' stats to mull over:

- 188 players are officially capped by the club.

- Of these, 105 have played ten or less games.

- There have been 63 different goalscorers

- Seb White holds the record for consecutive season appearances with 14, running from 1994/95 to 2007/08.

- 43 different players appeared during the 2000/01 season.

- During the same season, a club record 117 goals were scored.

- In 2004/05 Omer Kutluoglu had a strike rate of 138% with 18 goals in just 13 games. The following season he scored twenty in twenty one.

The following two pages will give you an insight into the club's recent history prior to my arrival and subsequent debut.

2002-2003 Season
West End (London) A.F.A. Sunday AM
First Division

		P	W	D	L	F	A	Pts
1	KXL Camden United	16	11	5	0	32	16	38
2	Heroes Of Waterloo	16	8	3	5	34	36	27
3	Churchill Arms	16	8	3	5	22	29	27
4	Catford Town	16	7	3	6	38	32	24
5	Original Black Stars	16	7	2	7	30	33	23
6	**Nice Fridge**	**16**	**7**	**1**	**8**	**28**	**35**	**22**
7	DFE	16	6	1	9	24	29	19
8	Kilburn Park	16	5	2	9	45	13	17
9	Nearly Athletic	16	2	2	12	15	45	8

Nearly Athletic	1	vs	2	Nice Fridge
KXL Camden United	1	vs	0	Nice Fridge
Kilburn Park	6	vs	2	Nice Fridge
DFE	4	vs	3	Nice Fridge
Churchill Arms	5	vs	0	Nice Fridge
Catford Town	Home win awarded			Nice Fridge
Heroes of Waterloo	2	vs	1	Nice Fridge
Original Black Stars	5	vs	0	Nice Fridge
Nice Fridge	3	vs	2	DFE
Nice Fridge	Home win awarded			Kilburn Park
Nice Fridge	0	vs	1	Original Black Stars
Nice Fridge	1	vs	1	KXL Camden United
Nice Fridge	6	vs	3	Catford Town
Nice Fridge	5	vs	3	Churchill Arms
Nice Fridge	3	vs	1	Heroes of Waterloo
Nice Fridge	2	vs	0	Nearly Athletic

2003-2004 Season

West End (London) A.F.A. Sunday AM

First Division

		P	W	D	L	F	A	Pts
1	Bethwin	13	12	1	0	30	11	37
2	Inter Chronic	14	9	1	4	46	19	28
3	Catford Town	14	8	3	3	35	18	27
4	Hyde Athletic	14	6	2	6	32	23	20
5	**Nice Fridge**	14	5	3	6	26	31	18
6	Pegasus	13	5	1	7	26	40	16
7	Tony's McGovern	14	3	1	10	20	37	10
8	Facile Tigre	14	1	0	13	16	52	3

Inter Chronic	2	vs	2	Nice Fridge
Nice Fridge	2	vs	3	Bethwin
Nice Fridge	1	vs	4	Tony's McGovern
Hyde Athletic	2	vs	1	Nice Fridge
Nice Fridge	Away win awarded		Inter Chronic
Catford Town	8	vs	2	Nice Fridge
Tony's McGovern	Away win awarded		Nice Fridge
Nice Fridge	2	vs	2	Hyde Athletic
Nice Fridge	5	vs	4	Facile Tigre
Nice Fridge	5	vs	3	Pegasus
Pegasus	1	vs	2	Nice Fridge
Nice Fridge	Draw awarded		Catford Town
Bethwin	2	vs	1	Nice Fridge
Facile Tigre	0	vs	3	Nice Fridge

Turkish Delight

The 2005/06 season was one of the most successful in the club's history, although it was pretty uneventful on the whole with only two matches really lasting in the memory. The first was definitely a significant low in my Nice Fridge career, with the other being somewhat better.

At the time the game was the biggest I had ever played in. We were up against Ferndale who were always in the running when it came to competing for the league title. The problem for us was that the title they regularly won was the Premier Division and we were very much a mid-table side in the First Division. We were most definitely the underdogs and, on-paper at least, were due an absolute hammering. One thing in our favour however, was the state of the pitch. The cup game was at Hurlingham meaning that the changing rooms were exceptional but the pitch was mediocre at best. It is incredibly narrow and even more incredibly bumpy. Within the first five minutes it was clear that Ferndale were very much out of their comfort zone. They were obviously used to pinging cross-field balls to one another and passing it along the back four, basically wearing the opposition down and pouncing when it was least expected. This was certainly not possible on the day – the passing was mis-placed and it was difficult for them to get a decent first touch. Us, on the other hand, were happy to stick to our route one, counter attacking football that we played no matter whether we were the underdogs or the favourites.

Unfortunately Ferndale did eventually get into their stride and it was pretty obvious that we were going to be up against it from there on in. However, our 4-5-1 formation soon changed to 5-5-0. There was no point looking to score at this stage, but if we could get through the first forty-five minutes without conceding, then anything could happen. Somehow, in true Nice Fridge fashion we created a chance on the counter-attack. The effort was blocked (their keeper still hadn't touched the ball) and went behind for a corner. Then came the miracle. Perhaps through complacency on their part, perhaps through tactical genius on ours, we had a spare man at the far post who rose majestically to nod the chance home. We were more shocked than they were! We didn't even really know how to celebrate. One thing we did know though was that it was now going to be even harder than before!

The rest of the game was exactly as expected. We didn't leave our half and for long periods of time didn't really leave our own penalty area. We defended like warriors, with Ferndale having nothing more than a few half-chances that were either easily saved or went aimlessly wide. They clearly didn't like teams soaking up the pressure. Then came one of the most embarrassing moments of my career (and probably my life) so far...

The final minute approached and Ferndale had the ball with their centre back. There was time for one last attack, as long as they went long with it... and they did. Maybe it was through the shock of seeing them launch the ball forward, maybe we were just all too tired, but we were caught out. Chris Ellis was out-muscled to the ball and the striker was through one-on-one with me. Now, at this point you would be forgiven for thinking that I made a complete fool of myself by falling over, or missing the ball, or scoring an own goal, but it was nothing of the sort. As you would expect at their level, the forward casually stroked the ball into the bottom corner and they all celebrated as if they had just won the Cup Final, not just equalised against the 'minnows.' Confused?

Well, as the players all embraced and made their way back to the halfway line, I was confronted by a small ten-year old boy who decided to pull the faces and make the noises that all ten-year olds tend to make when mocking somebody. Aren't they just so sweet?! Not surprisingly, at the time I was a bit dejected. We had come within second of beating a top class side and unfortunately my emotions got the better of me. I proceeded to chase the boy off of the pitch, calling him every name under the sun. The outcome? I didn't catch him and he spent the whole of extra-time wandering behind my goal and making random comments about how I liked chasing young boys! We eventually lost the game 4-2.

At the final whistle tensions were a bit fraught but the majority exchanged the traditional handshakes and wished one another good luck for the rest of the season. That is, except for one 'pleasant' individual who had travelled the entire length of the pitch just to come face to face with me. It was pretty obvious that he was the uncle of the boy that I had previously got to know quite well. How did I know this? Well it doesn't take Sherlock Holmes to work out what "why the f*ck did you chase my nephew" means, does it?

Fortunately, I was surrounded by a number of my team-mates and we all came up with a selection of random and mumbled excuses and apologies. Strangely, it seemed that they had worked, until he launched himself forward and head butted me straight on the cheek. The force of the impact, and potentially the glare of his three gold teeth, knocked me to the ground where I was very quickly and luckily surrounded by my team-mates again. The 'prat' as I affectionately refer to him, walked off and I was helped back to my feet. It genuinely hadn't hurt, but to say that I was shocked and shaken was an understatement. Omer and the ref came together and agreed that it would definitely be referred to the league and mentioned in the match report. At this point Omer chose to break some interesting news to us all:

"The league probably won't be that surprised to be honest" he proudly stated.

"Really? Surely it isn't a normal thing?" It seemed a reasonable question to ask.

"Oh, well I should have told you all this before, but I didn't want to worry you."

We all waited, in silence, for the punch line. Was this Omer's way of trying to cheer up the mood? Nope.

"Fernhdale are a team of ex-prisoners who have been put together by the league. Almost like a rehab team I suppose."

You suppose?!?! I had just chased and threatened the nephew of an ex-convict. There is every chance that he may have just been in prison for a number of traffic offences, but, at the same time, he may have been a mass murderer. Now wasn't the time to find out. I wanted to just get changed and go home.

I should explain at this point that the team had significantly changed from the days of my first few games. A number of the players had retired completely, but the majority had just limited themselves to half a dozen games a season. Whether that be due to fitness or the threats of divorce I wouldn't like to comment. Therefore, being the youngest in the side and still playing five-a-side football every Thursday with my mates back in Dartford, I was often asked to bring some along to make up the numbers. Just quickly, can I give a mention to that very successful five-a-side team, namely Dave FC, who took the Thursday Evening Dartford Goals League by storm. And, just for the record, our name came long before the channels Dave and Dave Ja Vu.

The previously mentioned Step and Pete Sharp, Chris Ellis, Ross Jenner, Carlos Sanchez, Rich Davis and Sameer Joomun all made appearances for Nice Fridge. Therefore, at times, eight of the squad for a West London side were travelling along the A2 and South Circular from Dartford, leaving at half eight in the morning for a 10:30am start. We, of coure, had to leave enough time for a McDonalds breakfast didn't we?

As well as the Division One league that we played in, there were also two cup competitions each season. One included all of the teams from our division as well as the division above (Challenge Cup) and the other was just for the teams in our league (Challenge Trophy). Both were straight knockout.

Apparently the draw for the Challenge Cup is completely random, but we always seem to come up against the Premier Division equivalent of Brazil – hence the head butting incident. The Challenge Trophy is obviously always a much closer and more exciting affair. In our division, no matter how the league table looked at the end of the season, anybody could beat anybody on their day – that's one of the thrills of Sunday League football. For some reason, this competition has always brought out the best in us and this year was no different. We found ourselves in the final, up against the best footballing side in the league; the Turkish team of Deportivo Atlas.

We had known this team for a few years and knew just how good they were. However, the strange thing was that we always tended to beat them, and often pretty comfortably. We actually suffered our first ever defeat to them the season before, when they beat us two-nil. Earlier on in the season though, we had produced one of our most emphatic performances ever. On a sloping Warren Farm pitch and with only ten men (thanks to me being able to recruit Ross at the last minute for his debut) we royally thumped them five-one. I have three incredible memories from the game – the first was Ross making up about twenty yards on their striker to clear a goal-bound effort off the line, the second was a 45yard screamer from Jez that rifled into the very top left corner of the goal and the third was a penalty save by yours truly. The save itself didn't mean a great deal in the context of the game, as we were already four up, but from a goalkeeping point of view there really is no better feeling.

Another incredible performance came in my one and only appearance at the famous Hackney Marshes. As kick off approached we only had ten men, one of whom was Pete with an ankle at least twice the size it should have been. It was also an interesting shade of green and blue, but we were short of players and there was no way that he was going to see the team play with just nine! Omer went on a quick scouting mission and returned with a seventeen year old going by the name of Scott. We had no idea if he was any good, but he certainly had the look of a Sunday league footballer.

Within the first five minutes of the game it was clear that Scott was average at best. I'm being slightly generous there, as he was in fact not far away from being completely useless. The problem was that he didn't know it. He genuinely thought that he was the next Fernando Torres. As expected, Deportivo had all of the ball and we were defending for our lives. The only strange thing was that I had nothing to do. They were adamant that the only way in which they wanted to score was by walking it into the back of the net, almost like Arsenal a few seasons ago. Anything from more than six yards just wasn't cricket!

As the game went on it was obvious that they were not going to score. The only question was whether we would. Finally, the breakthrough came and, yes you've guessed it, it came from the left foot of young Scott. As always, he backed his 'ability' and attempted to hit a volley from 25yards. We all groaned in unison, expecting it to either go out for a throw, trickle through to the keeper or hit the corner flag. What we didn't expect was for it to fly into the bottom right hand corner, leaving the goalkeeper absolutely helpless. He celebrated as if it was a regular event for him; we just laughed and got on with the game. We eventually won 2-0.

So, as I was saying, we certainly knew what to expect from them on Cup Final Day. The game was played at Hanwell Town Football Club, a 'real' ground with a clubhouse, changing rooms, dugouts, advertising boards, turnstiles, terraces and even a small seating area. This was a novelty to all of us, but we really wanted to make the most of it. In terms of quality, the changing rooms are on a similar level to those at Wormwood Scrubs, but the pitch, in comparison, was a carpet. A very large carpet. It's all well and good seeing a full-size pitch from the stand at The Valley or The Boleyn Ground (no, it's not called Upton Park!) but until you run onto one ready to play a game you don't quite appreciate the dimensions. If I'm honest, my ground kicking has never been that impressive, often struggling to reach the halfway line at South Park. There was absolutely no chance of me getting anywhere near that far here! Despite all of the apprehension and nerves, there was a sense of real excitement – after all, this was our Wembley.

The plan was to start in a 4-5-1 formation, soak up the early pressure and re-assess the situation after twenty minutes. It was soon clear that something had to be changed. The formation just wasn't working. There was only one thing for it – the famous 5-5-0. Once again, we would defend for our lives and worry about the idea of scoring when we got to half time. Then came another surprise. As the half-time whistle went, the Turks disappeared back to the changing rooms in a bit of a strop. We didn't know what to do – we had never had the opportunity of spending the interval under cover before. We were simply used to getting in a huddle around our bags behind the goal, having a chat and then swapping ends for the second half. So, some four or five years before Phil Brown's exploits at Eastlands, we stayed out and did precisely what we had done for every other game in the club's history. That being we spend five minutes talking about the game and what we needed to do and then found somebody to pick on for the remaining ten. Fortunately for me, but unfortunately for him, it was usually Jez on the receiving end.

The second half began with us in the same 5-5-0 setup that we had ended with some fifteen minutes before. Literally minutes later Deportivo had started their traditional demise. Whenever things didn't go their way, they invariably started to blame one another and were very vocal in doing so. Everything was said in Turkish so I really couldn't tell you the exact phrases, but I would imagine that if I had been taking notes I would now be fluent in Turkish insults and swear words. I probably wouldn't have learnt how to say 'have a nice day' though, which is a shame.

Realising that this could be our opportunity, we changed back to the 'attacking' 4-5-1 formation and it worked an absolute treat. Quicker than you can say 'amina koyayim' (maybe I did learn something, I'll let you look it up yourselves) we were four nil up! Four unanswered goals against the best team in the league, the best coming from the perfectly shaped shoulder of Carlos. Confidence was clearly so high that we were seeing what 'new' body parts could be used to score goals. Either that or Carlos mis-timed his jump and header and the ball merely hit him on the right shoulder and left their keeper stranded – make up your own minds.

Deportivo were so distraught that it really was a good thing when the final whistle went. Not only were we delighted to have won, but if it had gone on any longer, there is every chance that a Turkish Civil War may have broken out on the pitch. They had absolutely no interest in collecting their runners-up medals and went straight off to the changing rooms, got changed, got in their cars and drove off – still shouting at one another, obviously.

We really didn't care. No, it wasn't particularly sporting of them but it was testament to our performance on the day that had resulted in their reaction. It was certainly better for it to be this way round than having to watch them pick up the trophy. We all stayed in the clubhouse bar afterwards to celebrate what had been an incredible season. We had finished third in the league having lost only four games all season and had won the Challenge Trophy – an award that has since been re-named "Our Cup." In the same season, Chelsea won the Premier League, Man Utd the Carling Cup and Liverpool the FA Cup, meaning that we were more successful than both Arsenal and Spurs put together. You don't know how good it feels to be able to write that!

Deportivo and AFC Clapham were promoted to the Premier League at the end of the season. Following two years of steady progression, next year was going to be our big chance to push for the league title.

Mind Games

For some reason, the 2006/07 season didn't even come close to living up to expectations. By the time the Christmas break was upon us we had only picked up seven points out of a possible twenty one. The team was pretty much the same as it had been before and, if anything, the opposition were a lot weaker but something just wasn't working. The second half of the season was a complete mirror of the first, again only picking up a measly seven points out of twenty one. There was, however, always the Division One Challenge Cup to look forward to. The season had been a bizarre one and this cup campaign was to be no different.

With ten teams originally registered in the league it would be necessary for four teams to compete in two Preliminary Round matches in order to establish the Quarter Final line-up. As had been our luck throughout the season, we were one of the teams drawn out and were put up against Brazen United FC, the only team that had been relegated from the Premier Division and the stand-out favourites to take the Division One title this year.

The relegation however, had taken a big hit on the number of Brazen players who wanted to keep playing for the club and by the time our fixture had come round on 3rd December they had already dropped out of the league. Without even kicking a ball, we were in the draw for the Quarter Finals of 'our cup.'

We should have probably expected it, but we were given another tough draw in the form of Churchill Arms. Having already played them earlier on in the season, we knew what to expect and knew that it was going to be tough. They were a strong, physical side with big and powerful players at both ends of the pitch and had comfortably trounced us 5-2 in that encounter. One positive to take on board though was that they were not the quickest of sides and our counter-attacking football could work perfectly. The game, along with the other three quarter finals, was due to take place on 14th January but ours was the only one to fall foul of the delightful English weather. Our pitch was totally water-logged and without doubt unplayable –

the big question here is how (or where) the other three games managed to go ahead.

There would be an incredibly long wait for the game to be rescheduled. The league fixtures were already set in place for the rest of the year and it turned out that the next available slot would be Sunday 13th May, only two weeks before the final itself. In an ideal world we were going to have a Quarter Final, Semi Final and Final on three consecutive weekends. I say weekends, rather than Sundays as the Final had randomly been scheduled for the Bank Holiday Monday – at the time I assumed that the likes of Sky had managed to get it rearranged for live TV coverage. I was probably wrong.

Then came another shock – it made perfect sense with how the rest of our season had gone. The week of the game had approached and everybody was focused. That was, until Omer received a phone call. The draw had been made for the Semi Final and we were one win away from playing against our old friends Old Theonians. Just to clarify, I personally don't have any real affection with Theos but apparently the founders of both clubs had been good friends and there had been a good relationship ever since. We even had a game of cricket against them one summer which we comfortably won – a feat that is more impressive when I tell you that they have an actual cricket team and we opened our batting with Chris Ellis and Jez Mahon, simply on the basis that they hadn't bowled when we were fielding. There had been a very good reason for this however – neither are any good at cricket. I seem to remember them both getting out for a duck, but then so did I. Atleast I took three wickets with the ball though.

The following day Omer received another phone call (it's lucky that he owns a company and doesn't have to worry about explaining to anybody why he isn't doing any work!) but this time it was from Old Theos themselves. Surely they weren't starting the pre-match banter before we had even played our Quarter Final? They weren't. They supposedly had some bad news. They had already called Churchill Arms and we were next on their speed dial to be told that they were unable to get a team out for the Semi Final the following week. I know this sounds ridiculous, but this is one of the challenges of Sunday league football. With teams regularly made up by three or four groups of friends, it only takes one of these to have a stag-do, wedding, holiday etc and there is nothing you can do. Usually, certainly from a Nice Fridge point of view anyway, you try to sort out a rearranged date for the fixture – after all, everybody knows that it will happen to them at one stage and you hope that karma will work in your favour. However, in this instance we knew that this wasn't going to be possible. The Cup Final was the following week and there was simply no time for the game to be played. For a split second we almost felt sorry for Old Theonians (we were supposed to be friends, remember) and then it clicked that we were only ninety minutes away from another Cup Final. In fact, our one and only game in the competition so far was going to be our Semi Final!

After such an eventful week, the Quarter Final (officially) was played on a very boggy and wet pitch at Wormwood Scrubs and was nothing short of a classic. It was end-to-end from the first minute with both teams exchanging chances, blows and goals. With the game in its final third we found ourselves 3-2 behind and under a fair amount of pressure. There was no need to panic though. In times of trouble there was only one solution – route one. And it worked a treat. By the 85th minute we had turned the game on its head and were leading 4-3. As you would expect from a losing team at the end of a Semi Final (unofficially), Churchill Arms threw absolutely everything at us but we stayed solid. I made a couple of decent saves and there were a fair few last ditch challenges – it seemed as if we were going to hold on, until they won a corner with no more than 30 seconds left to play.

All twenty two players were in and around our penalty area as the cross came in. Their six foot five centre back (and captain) rose majestically from around the penalty spot and, due to his height and strength, effectively had a free header on goal. It was a bullet header and I was completely routed to my spot - there was absolutely no way I was getting anywhere near it. I knew however, that there was one last hope. Over the years Ross Jenner had given himself a reputation of being in the right place at the right time. This is no exaggeration but he has easily cleared twenty goal-bound efforts off of the line in his Fridge career. As he was so good at it, he always took my right hand post from set pieces – I would back myself to save most things going to my left, but the right was a different story.

There was no doubt that Ross would be there and be doing everything in his power to keep the ball out, but was the header going to have too much on it? He got himself air-bound and flung himself towards the ball. An inch or so shorter and Ross wouldn't have stood a chance but he somehow got the top of his head to the ball and diverted it upwards onto the underside of the cross-bar. As the ball came back down everything seemed to go into slow motion. Five or six players were charging and bundling forward but Ross composed himself and thumped the ball away and into touch. Churchill Arms were all celebrating. Either they appreciated the efforts of Ross as much as we did or they thought the ball had crossed the line. Then came a few seconds of tension and nerves. The ref blew his whistle and pointed to the halfway line. Absolute heartbreak – everything Ross and the team had done had been for nothing, we would have to play extra-time. That was my immediate reaction anyway, until the ref continued to blow his whistle and I realised that it was full time. He hadn't given the goal at all – we were once again in The Cup Final!

To say that Churchill Arms were angry would be an understatement. The scenes that followed were truly despicable and irresponsible. The players literally chased the ref off of the pitch and out of the ground. The poor sod didn't even have a chance to get changed, opting to go straight to the safe haven of his car. With one of the country's most secure prisons across the road, I wasn't sure that it was the best idea from a Churchill point of view, but more worryingly there were very few policemen around to come to the rescue. Saying that, I don't suppose anybody tends to risk committing a crime that close to Wormwood Scrubs! It is one of the few times that I have been genuinely disappointed and upset with the actions of an opposition (at least Deportivo just stormed off and argued amongst themselves) and I hope that all of their team looked back on it once they got home and realised how stupid they had been. I would also like to think that they eventually gave the ref an apology, but both are just as unlikely.

Enough of all this negativity – we were once again in 'our' Cup Final and had every intention of retaining the trophy. More importantly, it meant another visit to Hanwell Town. That was until we got the email saying that the game wouldn't be there, but at some random place called Broadfields in North Harrow. I had no idea where Broadfields was, mainly because I wasn't really sure where Harrow was. Despite the disappointment of it not being at Hanwell Town, we were still in the Cup Final and surely the ground would be just as good quality. The opposition? A Small World.

For unknown reasons, the Sunday Morning Challenge Trophy Final was scheduled to kick off at 2pm on Bank Holiday Monday. On driving into the car park it was clear that it wasn't in the same league as Hanwell – there was just a clubhouse and five or six pitches. The pitches did look impressive though, even if it had been a ridiculously wet weekend. There was a game in progress on one of the pitches in the corner so we chose the first one that we came across to warm-up on. Just for the record, a warm-up in Sunday League terms consists of every single outfield player pinging random twenty yard efforts at the keeper. The only problem with this, from my point of view at least, is that the goalkeeper is very much dependant on the standard of shooting. Two things can happen – either you get warmed up by diving or you get warmed up by running after wild efforts that have flown aimlessly wide.

Within five minutes of being on this pitch, we were politely asked to move. Apparently the groundsman would be very appreciative if we could have our kick-around in between the pitches so as not to ruin the goalmouth. My immediate reaction was to be very impressed by the professionalism of this setup but this was soon banished when we were called over to the pitch that we were going to playing the final on. Despite all of the other surfaces doing their best Highbury impressions, they had decided that all of the WELAFA Cup Finals would be played on the same pitch. I imagine that even this had been like a carpet on Saturday morning, but five games and torrential rain later it was closer to that of an African swamp. There were puddles everywhere and grass nowhere.

The rain came down as soon as the game kicked off and it was anything but a pretty contest. Both teams were aggressive and physical with one another and the ref didn't really know what to do. The conditions meant that most tackles were poorly timed and chances were limited. It was nil nil at half time with very little to talk about. The second half, on the other hand, certainly made up for the poor start. ASW soon took a deserved two goal lead and continued to come forward looking to kill off the game and inflict our first defeat in the competition for almost two years. If you haven't worked it out already though, this Nice Fridge team do not know when they are beaten and by the time the full time whistle was blown we had pulled it back to two all, the highlight being another Jez thunderbolt. This time he picked the ball up from all of thirty yards and let rip with an effort that can only be described as ambitious. The keeper? Absolutely no chance! Extra time came and went pretty quickly. To be honest, both teams were shattered and had, it seemed, already decided on letting it go to penalties.

Neither goalmouth was in particularly good condition, but one was significantly better than the other. The ref obviously didn't see it like this though and chose the worse of the two – all I can assume is that his decision was based on the fact there was a fence behind the goal. He clearly didn't have a lot of confidence in us.

If the story of me chasing a ten year old boy was a significant low in my career, then this is without doubt the most embarrassing. I would love to deny every bit of what you are about to read but all of it was perfectly recorded on a video camera by Step and Pete's dad. What makes it worse is that he also made it into a DVD which tends to get shown two or three times a year – thanks Ian!

As everybody knows, a penalty shoot-out is a no lose situation for a goalkeeper. If it goes his way then he is a hero, if it doesn't then people only remember the guy who missed the decisive penalty. For the first two kicks I dived to my left and was sent the wrong way for both. I dived right for the next penalty and was again sent the wrong way – except the ref demanded that this was retaken as the penalty taker had struck the ball before the whistle had been blown. I tried to out-think the striker here and changed my previous direction, going back to my original plan of diving left. He went to my right. 3-3 with six very confident penalties. The next three penalties were also scored, with me diving to my left again for my two and being sent the wrong way for both – again! We were 5-4 down with Ross making the long walk from the halfway line, knowing that he had no option but to score. I was nervous to say the least. Ross may have been good at defending and clearing balls off of the line but I wasn't sure if I had ever seen him take a penalty.

He got to the end of his run-up and the whole ground fell silent. As he approached the ball in his typical casual style, I could hardly look. He stroked it with the inside of his right foot to the keeper's left. It was heading right into the corner but their keeper was making up the ground quickly. The lack of pace on the kick had given their goalkeeper every chance and he pounced across to tip the ball away. A Small World all sprinted towards the goal cheering and celebrating. We had lost the game. We had lost 'our cup.'

The ref was blowing his whistle like a madman and the linesman appeared to be doing some sort of Morris Dance. Now didn't seem the right time to be joining in with the winning team's celebrations. But they weren't. The linesman had judged that their keeper had stepped off of his line before the ball was struck. It seemed harsh, as there is not a keeper in the World who stays on his line for a penalty, but we certainly weren't going to complain. The opposition, on the other hand, were not so keen on the decision. After a few minutes of, shall we say, friendly discussions, the penalty shootout continued and Ross was ready to try again. Once again, Ross hit the weakest of penalties I have ever seen. It was a spitting image of his last one, except this time the keeper had gone the other way. Due to the conditions of the pitch it was touch and go at one stage as to whether it would cross the line, but eventually it nestled into the net, no more than two inches from the inside of the post. 5-5.

    I could sense my chance. I could make myself a real hero in the next five minutes and win us the cup. As their striker stepped forward I eyed up his body language and position. I knew exactly where he was going – it couldn't have been more blatant. I threw myself to my left. He rolled the ball into the bottom right hand corner. Bugger! 6-5 to them.

    It is at this stage of any shootout that the 'not so confident' players are called upon and this was no different - up stepped Mr Chris Ellis. In complete contrast to Ross, Chris certainly isn't renowned for his subtlety and there was only one way that this penalty was going to be taken - foot through it, as hard as physically possible. The only doubt was where the ball would end up. All he had to do was hit the target. How would the keeper know where he was going to put it, if he had no idea himself? The minute or so that followed was absolute torture, but I need not have worried. As Stuart Pearce had done some ten years earlier in Euro 96, Chris let out every last bit of energy and emotion and fired the ball into the top right corner. It was simply unstoppable. It was Pearce-esque but Alan Shearer would have been proud of it. 6-6.

    At this rate we were going to be here all night. Once again, I set myself ready for the penalty and did my best to put off their player. For the first time in the shootout I also had a number of my team shouting at me from the halfway line.

> "What about diving the other way?"
> "Dive right you twat"
> "Go to your f*cking right!"

You get the idea.

I was now in a difficult situation. Their player had obviously heard all of it and would have been thinking the same as me. I had gone left for all six of the previous penalties, so did I do the same again or did I change my mind? What did he think I was going to do? I weighed up my options and took all of the comments on board and, most importantly, made up my decision early. I dived left (obviously) and he put his penalty... to my right (obviously). The problem for him though was that he put his penalty very right and it sailed aimlessly past the post. We were one kick away from getting our hands back on that trophy.

Up stepped Martinez and I had never been more confident about somebody scoring from the point. He was our magician winger who would just run and run and run. Once, he cycled to a game, played ninety minutes at full pace and then cycled off to compete in a Triathlon across the other side of London. Impressive, yes. Insane, even more so!

As expected, Martinez fired the ball into the back of the net and the crowds went wild. The whole team charged forward towards him, pretty much knocking him to the ground in their excitement. I decided to stay out of it. I couldn't really take any credit for this victory. Just for the record, Martinez is now living happily in Chamonix – I'd imagine telling every tourist that he comes across of this incredible story. Or running up and down a mountain. Probably both.

Omer then did a very kind and generous thing – he gave me the honour of collecting the trophy and raising it aloft on behalf of the club. I was genuinely speechless and proud, so much so that I clearly forgot how to smile. If you see the photos from the presentation there is only one thing that you notice. It's not the trophy, it's not the fact that I was literally dripping with mud, but the ridiculous facial expression that I have chosen to pull. If it hadn't been for the events leading up to this moment then I would, in hindsight, feel pretty daft and stupid.

Fortunately, all was forgotten relatively quickly. As soon as we were changed and dried off, we found ourselves in the bar celebrating a second consecutive cup triumph. It wasn't Hanwell Town, but it would certainly do!

The Russian Revolution

On the back of two successive cup winning seasons, it was going to take something magic to top it this year. However, the 2007/08 campaign would go down in the record books as one of the most important in the Club's relatively short history. In terms of league performance it really wasn't going to take much to improve on our measly fourteen points, but trying to retain the Challenge Cup AGAIN was going to be even harder. As any sportsman knows, the longer somebody goes undefeated, the more your next opposition want to take the achievement away from you.

Before we could even let this cross our minds, Omer wrote an email that must have sent shockwaves across the whole of London. Nice Fridge Football Club was in advanced discussions with Locomotiv Knightsbridge Football Club over the possible merger of the two clubs. None of us had ever heard of them and I can't imagine their situation was any different. Where had this suddenly come from and what did it mean for the future of the club? For me, something didn't feel right. That name meant something, but I couldn't work out why. Then it clicked – all them years ago when I had misunderstood what Jez had said the team was called. Either, one of us was able to see into the future or it was an incredible coincidence. Whatever one of the two it was, it seemed like it was meant to be and that the two sides had always been destined to come together.

Everything went quiet on the 'takeover' until the morning of our first pre-season friendly. It seemed that everything had been finalised at the eleventh hour and a new club had been formed. From this day forward we would be known as Nice Fridge Locomotiv. The squad split was fairly even, with about twelve from Nice Fridge and ten from Locomotiv. Unfortunately, the performance on the pitch wasn't quite as smooth.

Despite having a new green and white hooped kit, which I assume Locomotiv had worn before, we may as well have still been in our red and blue strip. Tim Lovejoy and Jeff Stelling always joke about Dagenham and Redbridge vs Anybody Else as a three-way battle and this was probably as close to this as you are ever likely to get. The opposition must have been so confused.

Now, I'm by no means saying that what happened was deliberate on anybodies part but, subconsciously at least, Nice Fridge would only pass to Nice Fridge and Locomotiv would only pass to Locomotiv. In the squad's defence, it is hard enough to feel settled when there are just one or two newcomers on the pitch so it must have been near-on impossible with half a team of complete strangers. However, the only logical way to turn a stranger into a non-stranger is by interacting and communicating with them – something that Omer did not hold back in explaining to the team at half time. I had never seen him lose his temper before and it was certainly an experience to have a relatively posh chap swearing and shouting, but still managing to keep it reasonably polite. How that is possible, I'm not sure, but he managed it somehow and we even put in a decent performance for the second half.

Over the next few weeks though, it was clear that some of the Locomotiv players hadn't taken too kindly to this method of management and, before long, we were down to just five of them - Shane, Matty, Neil, Martin and Lance. It wasn't long until this became four and, although it has never been confirmed, I am pretty sure that it was Omer's responsibility again. In his defence the first few weeks of the season had been very frustrating with a number of players dropping out on the Saturday night before the game, often leaving us with a bare eleven.

It was a complete novelty, therefore, when nobody had given Omer an awful excuse and we were due to have a squad of twelve for the game against the league leaders. As always we had agreed to meet at the changing rooms at 10am, leaving enough time to get changed and have a quick warm-up. Twenty past ten approached and there were still only nine of us. We were missing Jez and Lance. Both the ref and the opposition were getting anxious to start but we managed to delay them by fifteen minutes. Fifteen pointless minutes I might add. Neither turned up and we had no choice but to play the game with ten men. We were beaten 3-2 with at least two of the goals being my fault, but, once again I had chosen the right game to play badly. There were more serious issues to be resolved and I got away with it!

The match report and a very stroppy email were waiting for us all the following morning. Omer had set a new rule that if you were in the squad and simply didn't turn up then you would still be charged subs for the game. He was also keen to hear the thoughts and excuses from the AWOL pair. Jez, in his defence, came back immediately and apologised to everybody. He didn't have a decent excuse and was prepared to admit it. Basically, he had been out the night before, one thing had led to another and he had completely slept through his alarm. It wasn't ideal, but the honesty was certainly appreciated. He promised that it wouldn't happen again and was left to wash the kit for the next few weeks.

A reply from Lance came a few days later. He had been called to Munich with his work at the last minute on Saturday night and had only just got home. He hadn't had a chance to get to his emails and didn't have Omer's number to call him and let him know. I got the impression that Omer didn't know whether to apologise or to stick by his original hair-dryer approach. Lance, on the other hand, clearly hadn't taken the email too kindly. I personally don't think that he ever completely settled himself into the side and that this was just the excuse he needed, but we never saw him again!

Within six weeks of the famous merger it was basically Nice Fridge, plus four. But what a quartet they were. Shane was your typical Sunday League midfielder – a battling warrior that took command of the pitch, got stuck into every tackle and never gave up. Matty was his perfect companion – a creative midfielder, with a great first touch, superb vision and incredibly awareness. If Shane was your Roy Keane (he was Irish, after all) then Matty was Paul Scholes. Martin had the flexibility of being able to play either on the wing or as a centre forward. He had the strength and presence to be a lone striker, but also had the skill and pace to take defenders on down the line. He also had a throw that would rival the very best that Rory Delap has to offer. Neil completed the quartet and brought an incredible football brain to the side, along with a never-before-seen level of professionalism and the capability of holding together both the defence and midfield.

We now had a committed group of players that soon saw the results and performances go our way. We also had two brand new kits. The aforementioned Celtic-like strip was one and the other was navy blue and red – impressively, it was made by Nike. There was one catch though. The goalkeeper shirt, also Nike, was somewhat large. It was, in fact, an XXL.

Colin Gibson and Seb White had a better idea. The following week they turned up and charged into the changing rooms with a plastic bag under their arm. What were they up to?

"Here, we have a present for you!" They said in their typically polite tones
"What... what is it?" I was genuinely worried.
"It's a new goalkeeper top for you"
"... Oh... OK... Thanks" I was now petrified.

Knowing Colin and Seb it would probably be a monkey outfit or something similar. To their credit, and I probably therefore owe them an apology, they pulled out a genuine goalkeeper's jersey. I have always been a fan of brightly coloured football shirts so was even more pleased to see that it was bright yellow, with a bold Premier League endorsed number one on the back. Then it struck me. As I turned it round I could see that it had a Wigan badge on. I have absolutely nothing against Wigan but it certainly wasn't what I was expecting.
They then proceeded to tell me the story of how this top had been worn by the Wigan goalkeeper Chris Kirkland just a few weeks before. At first I just laughed them off assuming they were joking around but then it became very clear that they were being deadly serious. They had genuinely got their hands on what could only be described as a piece of football memorabilia and decided to give it to me. And then the story continued even more...

"So how did you manage to get it then?" I enquired
"Well we were at a charity auction that was being run by some friends and the shirt was one of the lots." They proudly boasted
"And you thought you would just randomly bid on it for me?"
"No no no." They laughed. "It was the only item that didn't get a single bid and my friend just told me to get rid of it... so we thought of you."

I didn't know whether to be honoured, offended or something in between. It was kind of them to think of me, but was there a reason that I came to mind when they were effectively handed a piece of worthless rubbish? It didn't really matter – I had been given something that had been worn by a future England player. More importantly, I now had a top that did actually fit me. Even if it did have a Wigan badge on.

Deep down, I knew that it was Colin's way of apologising to me for a certain incident that happened in my second season. I had the misfortune of finding out just how strong and solid a centre back he actually was. I don't remember a great deal about the game anymore but can still very clearly see Colin sliding in towards me, as I was sliding out. We were both trying to dispossess the striker of the ball as he closed down on goal, only for us to carry on into one another. Colin's head went straight into mine and there was only going to be one winner. He got up (apparently) as if nothing had happened whereas I was rolling around in absolute agony (again, apparently because I don't really remember this bit). The next thing I knew was that I couldn't see out of my left eye – not because of any damage to it but because the skin above my eyebrow had swollen up so much that it was actually hanging over the eye itself. The score at the time was two one to us.

I spent the next two hours up at Accident and Emergency although, to this day, I still couldn't tell you which one I was in. I had been taken there on my own in an ambulance so was sitting in the waiting room with a thumping headache, balloon-sized head and in a dirty football kit. I must have been a right sight! Just as I was called in by the nurse Ross and Jez turned up. Before being checked over, I had to find out how the game had finished.

"We lost three two" said Jez depressingly

"But how? We were all over them! What happened?" I slurred (apparently)

"Omer went in goal…" Ross replied with a sense of anger.

"That explains it then… I'll be back in a bit."

With that I wobbled off into the cubical with the nurse and spent the next ten minutes having my head prodded and poked by an over-enthusiastic medical student. It turned out that I had suffered an ever-so-slight hairline fracture from my scalp down to my eyebrow but that it wouldn't cause any serious problems in the long-term. I do however, still get a sharp pain today if I ever put pressure on my left eyebrow. Simple solution – don't push my left eyebrow. It really hasn't caused that much of a lifestyle change. I just make sure that I am not in the same room as Colin.

Colin has since announced his retirement from Nice Fridge Locomotiv Football Club. Making his debut at the turn of the century (that's 2000 not 1900 just to clear up any potential confusion) he made a fine 87 appearances, scoring just the single goal. I bet it was a bullet of a header though!

Not only will he go down as a club legend but he is also one of the most pleasant players you could play with or against. As a team-mate he was always supportive and you knew that you were guaranteed to get 110% out of him every week. He must have been a nightmare to play against though, as he didn't give an inch, but did still find time to have a laugh and a joke with the opposition striker at set-pieces. He was the ultimate professional that no club could ever replace.

Don't We Know You From Somewhere?

A number of rivalries had been born in the Club's relatively short history, but perhaps the most significant started at the beginning of the 2007/08 season. When I say at the beginning, I actually mean during the pre-season. I appreciate that most normal rivalries are not created when it is supposedly a time for friendlies, but this would be no normal rivalry.

Every summer, around July time, the WELAFA League have their AGM where all representative teams come together to discuss the previous season and decide on any new rules and regulations for the year ahead. It is also a time for any new teams to register their interest in becoming a member. To be honest, it is more of one of them legal things that have to be done instead or something that necessarily achieves anything.

Omer turned up as normal, only to come in contact with a number of familiar faces. In front of him stood Graham, Pete and Ollie – three players that had played for us over the last few seasons. Graham was originally introduced to the team by Jez and then brought along Pete and Ollie to forthcoming games when we were short of players etc. At first you would be forgiven for thinking that they were there to give Omer a heroic welcome, but that wasn't the case. They were in fact registering a new team that would go by the name of The Ship – nobody had anything against them for 'going it alone' but it was the way that it had been done so secretly that just seemed to hit a nerve.

As any football fan will know, the so-called random fixture generator always tends to throw up an interesting game early on in the season. Whether it be a player going back to his former club or a manager doing the same there is always that added bit of spice. Our first home game of the season was, you guessed it, against The Ship. I have absolutely no idea how they approached the game or whether they saw it as a new rivalry but it didn't take much in the way of a team talk from Omer to get us in the right frame of mind. I therefore have great pleasure in saying that we thumped them four-one, despite conceding an early goal. Whether it was because they were a new team or whether they were just genuinely mediocre, it was clear that they only had one player with any real talent. The others were solid Sunday League players, but nothing more.

The next time that we met wasn't until reasonably late in the season. We had played ten games so far and hadn't been defeated. Despite four of them games ending in draws, we were still sitting fairly high in the league. This game, however, certainly wasn't going to be remembered for the performance, the football or the result. To give you an idea early on, it was without a doubt the worst performance by a referee that I have ever witnessed. I have experienced the idiocy of Graham Poll and the ridiculously arrogant Rob Styles on a number of occasions and neither of them even come close to what we had to put up with.

For starters, the ref looked as if he was no older than twelve. We had already had him for a few games earlier on in the year and he was nothing short of dreadful then. Perhaps realising that we were not his biggest fans, he came and had a chat with us before kick-off. Apparently, one of the referee assessors was there to watch him and he would appreciate it if we could work with him and make his life easier. We promised to do our best – in hindsight, if we had known, at this point, what was to follow then I don't think an agreement would have been made. Just for the record, the reason that he wasn't on our Christmas card list was that in our three previous encounters he had given no less than six penalties. Sunday league football will always be prone to more spot-kicks than your typical professional game, but an average of one every forty five minutes was just a little bit extreme.

One thing that did go against the referee was the type of match that he was officiating. It was never going to be the friendliest of games, not that there was anything malicious or aggressive going on either though. Both teams wanted to win the game – we were both near the top of the league, not to mention the added extra with the rivalry.

Then it began. The game had been fairly even with neither side creating anything more than a few half chances. The defences were definitely on top, which makes the following even more ridiculous. A long-field ball came into our penalty area with Rich Davis and their striker both battling for it. Just to put this into context, I had spent the last five years of my life trying to get Rich to stay on his feet when it came to defending. He was a strong, tall centre back who won everything in the air, but when it came to anything along the ground he was certainly prone to a badly timed sliding tackle.

I was screaming at him not to dive in but there really wasn't any point. He had already committed to the lunge and it was going to be very close as to whether he got to the ball first or not. By some miracle, Rich had timed it to absolute perfection – it was one of the best challenges that I had ever seen. Even their striker got to his feet and congratulated Rich before going to collect the ball to take the resulting corner. However, by the time he had recovered the football, the ref had blown his whistle and was pointing to the penalty spot. An outrageous piece of decision making and judgement had led to him giving The Ship a penalty. There were twenty two absolutely bewildered players – eleven were fuming, eleven couldn't stop laughing!

It must have taken at least five minutes to calm the situation down. Omer, Rich, Shane and I had all made our thoughts known to the ref but he was having none of it. The spot-kick was eventually taken and scored (I dived to my left) which resulted in a certain goalkeeper kicking the ball in the general direction of the official and calling him a "f*cking disgrace." Not surprisingly, he quickly produced the yellow card. It was my first ever booking and, to this day, something that I am still reasonably proud of. My parents have always brought me up to not tell lies, so why was I being punished for merely stating a fact?

For the rest of the game we were honestly and fairly outplayed… as far as the opposition were concerned anyway. The Ship were not at fault but the ref didn't give a single correct decision. He seemed to have a rule that he would blow his whistle for every coming together – the only problem was that it appeared he was simply guessing as to which way to give the decision. It's not even as if all of the free-kicks went against us. Over the course of the game it probably evened itself out, it was just the 50% that we should have had were given to them and vice versa.

We had lost all of our focus with the game and were only interested in making our feelings known to our new 'best friend.' Then came one of the funniest things I have ever seen on a football pitch. Shane had gone in for a tackle on the halfway line and again won the ball cleanly. The ref not only gave the free-kick against him but also produced another yellow card, citing persistent fouling. In his rage, Shane simply laughed and ripped the card out of the ref's hand

and threw it to the floor. In fairness, there was now only going to be one outcome – that yellow was quickly replaced by a red. The final decision couldn't be argued with but how it had come about certainly could.

Shane slowly left the field of play mixing up his swearing with fits of laughter. What we didn't realise at this stage was that Shane must have been planning his next move. Once behind the goal near me, he called over to the ref that we wanted to make a substitution. In football, a substitution after a sending off is fairly common but I am very confident that this has never happened before. The ref looked over and signalled that we could go ahead with the change, only to see Shane jog back onto the field of play with a huge grin on his face. Both teams thought it was hilarious, but the ref had clearly lost his sense of humour. He forced Shane back off and subsequently filed a report that led to a three month suspension. A small price for a pure act of genius!

The game again finished 4-1, except that this time we were on the receiving end. Considering the size of the defeat to our biggest rivals it just didn't seem that important - both sides agreed to put in a formal complaint against the official… maybe the rivalry wasn't that strong. That referee was never seen at a WELAFA game again. Whether he was 'fired' or whether he simply decided that enough was enough I do not know – quite frankly, I don't care either!

Other than the two league games, we were also drawn away to The Ship in the Semi-Final of 'our Cup.' We unfortunately lost this three-two to a last minute winner and with our undefeated run coming to an end, it is probably no great surprise that I have managed to erase the events of the match itself from my memory.

Over the course of the 2007/08 season we only played The Ship on the three occasions mentioned above. However, if you include our postponed matches, we met up on no fewer than seven Sunday mornings. The first 'attempt' was on Sunday 4th November 2007. We all turned up at the ground to find that the pitch was covered in beer cans, rubbish, bottles… and fireworks. After many arguments between the sides it was reluctantly agreed that the game would have to be called off. At a later date it was revealed that The Ship had been unable to get a pitch booked for our game, so, knowing that the park was being used for the Annual Fireworks Display the night before, they had told us of the location in order for us to 'see for ourselves.' It was too late to do anything about it, but the frustrating thing was that if they had told us the truth we would have agreed to rearrange the game and saved twenty two players the unnecessary journey.

The next bit of dishonesty on their part came just a few weeks into the New Year. We were due to play them at Boston Manor, which is miles away from any of us. Due to the distance involved, our Dartford group had to leave at about 8am and we were well and truly on our way when a phone call came in at 9am to say that the game was off due to a waterlogged pitch. It had been a relatively wet week, but nothing compared to others over the winter months. It was agreed that we would go to the ground anyway, just to have a kick-around for an hour or so. On arrival, something didn't seem right. There was no denying that it had been raining, but there certainly wasn't any standing water. They had again come up with an excuse to get the game called off!

A few weeks later however, we did get our own bit of revenge. Scheduled to be playing on the 'fireworks pitch' again we had been struggling for players all week. We eventually mustered up a bare eleven, only for three to drop out over the course of the weekend – it was too late to postpone so it was simply a case of making our way to the ground whilst making as many frantic calls as possible.

This achieved absolutely nothing. Nobody was available, nobody actually answered their phone. To be fair, if you don't have a reason to be up at 8am on a Sunday morning, it is very unlikely that you will be. When we got to the changing rooms it was clear that there were a few puddles of standing water on the pitch – a small one in the centre circle and two even smaller ones in both penalty areas. And then the ref turned up – it was an old Club friend.

It was agreed that we wouldn't mention the lack of players but would in fact run over to him before he got to the changing rooms and express our concerns over the conditions and the knock-on effect that this would have on the player's safety. Neither the ref nor The Ship were convinced. We did persevere though stating that none of our team should be made to play when there was a serious risk of injury, especially as this could mean time off work and not being able to pay the bills. Looking back it really was quite a pathetic sob story but miraculously it worked. Apparently the ref had suffered a similar fate many years ago and could see our point of view... what are the chances?

As we walked back to the changing rooms grinning like Cheshire cats the news spread to both sets of players. The Ship weren't particularly happy and their mood was made even worse when we explained that it was in fact a bonus for us, as we only had eight players. You could literally see their faces drop as we stepped past them and offered a friendly goodbye. Karma is a funny old thing.

The final rendezvous was once again down to poor organisation and management on their part. There is nothing particularly humorous or entertaining with this story but they simply failed to book a pitch again. Their manager thought that the secretary had done so and vice versa. So when we arrived to find all pitches being played on, they went for a quick hunt to see what they could find. The best they could do was a school pitch that was only half the normal size, with goals only slightly larger than five-a-side ones. Put it this way, the pitch was so miniscule that my goal kicks reached the other penalty area! The friendly game that we played was actually quite entertaining, but this didn't take away the fact that The Ship had royally messed up again.

Despite all of their inefficiencies off the field they had turned into a very good side. They had decided to drop one of their co-founders, Graham, from the side and I can say with some confidence that their improved performances were certainly connected to this decision. They subsequently won the league that season and were promoted into the Premier Division, meaning that we have not seen or played them since. I can point out, with some joy, that they finished rock bottom the following year and then moved to a different league all together, where they again finished bottom – I don't think they actually won a single game all season. My heart bleeds!

How Hard Can It Be?

I didn't know this yet, but the 2008/09 season would become the most significant in my short football career so far. It started fairly uneventfully with us, in typical Nice Fridge fashion, playing well and beating the good teams and then putting on dreadful performances against those near the bottom of the table. It was something that you just got used to when playing for the club but it didn't make it any less frustrating.

If I am honest, I had actually started to get bored. Not with the club and certainly not with football itself, but a typical Sunday would involve getting up at half seven in the morning and not getting home until around two in the afternoon. I was then usually so tired that I had no energy or enthusiasm to do anything for the rest of the day. On a personal level I had also just put a deposit down on my first flat with my now-fiancé and maybe it was time just to reassess the situation in general. Before anybody asks, Louisa didn't put any pressure on me to stop playing. If anything it was the complete opposite, as it meant she could stay in bed until gone lunchtime!

Around March-time I emailed Omer and asked for his advice. I didn't mention any of the above but said that I was interested in doing either the coaching or referee qualification. What he didn't know at this stage (and possibly didn't at all until now) was that I had been offered a number of trials by County-level clubs that were local to me. These weren't until the Summer but I figured that if I could get some sort of qualification under my belt beforehand then it would certainly make the transition up the league ladder that much easier.

Within minutes he replied to say that he could only see me being a coach. Despite my high knowledge of some of the more intricate rule details we both agreed that I probably didn't have the confidence or the presence to take control of a game of football. It would be OK when things were going well, but as soon as things turned slightly there would be every chance that I would be bullied into decisions and effectively eaten alive.

The only catch with becoming a qualified coach is the process in which it happens. In order to get to the very top, and by top I mean

Manchester United and Barcelona coaching levels, you need to complete four stages. Let's be honest, as good as it would be, I had no realistic chance or ambition of getting to this level so, for me, there were only really two. They are imaginatively named FA Coaching Level One and FA Coaching Level Two, with the others being the more famous UEFA B and UEFA A licenses. The other two things to take into consideration are the price and availability. It is hard enough to find a course that is reasonably local to you in the first place, but when you do you then tend to get the news that it has been fully booked for months and that the next one isn't until 2025. Which could work in my favour, as it should give me enough time to save up the funds – the first course is roughly £150, with Level Two rising to the region of £300. The UEFA courses are in their thousands!! On paper the first two prices do not sound that steep, but you try convincing your partner (and mortgage company) that you want to spend your wages on a course that teaches you more about football and you will see what I mean. I actually wrote a letter to the FA this Summer expressing my disappointment with the pricing structure and queried how they could expect the game to move forward, especially in light of the recent World Cup failings, with so many people being priced out. The response I received basically said "thank you very much for your letter, now go away and leave us alone!"

Always thinking though, Omer had an idea. Why spend that sort of money when I didn't know if I would actually enjoy it? It pains me to say it, but he had a point. He was going to be away for the weekend and needed somebody to take up the reigns, so it would be perfect! It was a Mickey Mouse Cup game so it didn't even matter if it went horribly wrong. Not that it would though; I knew all the players really well and was sure that they would make it as easy as possible for me.

"Thanks Omer, who are we playing?" Every good manager should know who his opposition are. I was already thinking like a professional.

"North Acton. They won the league last year!" Why was he smiling?

"But I thought The Ship ended up top?" I retorted

"They did. North Acton won the Premier Division. Good luck!"

Right then. The best team in the whole of the league ladder against the most inexperienced manager in Sunday league history. As I say, fortunately for me, it was literally a Mickey Mouse competition. The league always plan for a number of games to get postponed due to the weather etc so tend to leave things free from March onwards. However, there had been very few cancelled games this term so all leagues were all-but wrapped up by the time April came round. A random Invitational Cup Competition was therefore invented with four groups of four, each consisting of two teams from the Premier Division and two from ours.

The morning of the game arrived and I was fortunate enough to have a number of old-heads in the squad. The most notable of these was Colin Gibson. As previously explained, Colin is a club legend with ample experience and I knew that he would help me out. The other was Neil, somebody that seemed to have a ridiculous number of connections with Sunderland Football Club but also knew what he was talking about. The plan for the game? Make sure it did not end up a cricket score!

After ten minutes I realised that there was only thing harder than being a manager and that was being a player-manager, especially when that player was a goalkeeper. You would think that being in goal would give you a perfect view of the whole pitch, allowing you to see exactly what was going on, but you would be wrong. Although not always involved in play, a goalkeeper must be two minutes ahead of the game, preparing his defenders for anything that could potentially happen next. You are basically the equivalent of a chess player, the only difference being that football is a real sport.

Half time arrived and we found ourselves two-nil down. They had obviously been the dominate side but we had definitely not made it easy for them. Everyone huddled together and stared at me. What were they all expecting? I had absolutely no idea what to say. I had spent most of the half diving around or preparing my defenders for corners, but other than that had next to no idea of what had gone on. Thankfully Neil could see my problem and happily took control of the situation. It was agreed that, realistically, the game was probably lost, so we would start the second half as if it was a new match and see what happened.

Colin, on the other hand, didn't like this idea. He had been groomed with the Fridge mentally that a game is not over until the full time whistle goes. He explained that we had played against better teams in the past and come away with a result and that this should be no different. Fortunately, the ref then blew his whistle for the teams to come back onto the field so no further discussions took place.

Mr Gibson was clearly a genius. What he had said had obviously worked – all ten outfield players were chasing down the ball, winning the tackles and making North Acton look very ordinary. We were soon rewarded with a bit of luck. Probably due to complacency, their defenders were happy to pass the ball around their backline, trying unnecessary turns and such like that achieved nothing. Pete put pressure on the 'new-Ronaldo' (not the fat one) and forced him into a mistake. A short back pass was easily intercepted and Pete casually rounded the keeper to slot the ball into an empty net.

Next up was a moment of pure magic. We won a free-kick some twenty five yards out, just to the right of the goal. It was crying out for a shot. Unfortunately, there are no official stats on this game (that was probably something that I was supposed to do at the time) but I seem to remember Jez putting his full body weight into the shot and it screaming into the top right hand corner leaving the keeper helpless. I appreciate that it doesn't really sound like the sort of thing you would expect Jez to do, but I'm pretty sure it was him. We had done it! We had pulled it back to 2-2.

Unfortunately, it wasn't meant to be. With the clock ticking past the ninetieth minute North Acton had time for one last attack. Their striker had taken on a number of our players and was closing in on goal with only Step and myself in front of him. To this day, Step still regrets not taking the guy out before he got to the penalty area and he calmly slotted the ball across me into the bottom left hand corner. I believe that my first ever match report was entitled "Heartbreak At Hurlingham."

As the season went on, the remaining games were shared amongst Omer, Shane and myself. Soon after, Shane announced that he had been given a job back in Ireland and had no choice but to retire from Nice Fridge Locomotiv Football Club, leaving the responsibility to just the two of us. It didn't take long for Omer to then ask me if I wanted to take the job on a full-time basis. Basically, he was moving house and had just started a family so didn't want the added burden of running everything behind the scenes. My options were fairly simple – say yes, or say no and tell twenty players that the team they had been with for years no longer existed. Did I have a choice?

My biggest concern was the financial side of things. Without going into details Omer isn't short of a few pennies and had always been able to pay any costs upfront and then get them back from the players over the course of the season. I, unfortunately, am not in the same boat. The only way it could work would be if we all agreed to pay some subs at the start of the season, then topped them up at Christmas and did the same again come April/May time. Omer assured me that everybody would be fine with this as they would simply be grateful of my efforts to keep the club going. He certainly knew how to talk a load of rubbish.

The other agreement was that Omer would be responsible for all pre-season paperwork so that I was ready to go for the curtain-raiser in September. What actually took place was slightly different. Within a matter of days the HSBC bank details, the pitch bookings and the league secretary contacts were all changed into my name and address. I must not forget though that he did pay the £16 for the Public Liability Insurance – he hadn't completely left me in the lurch!

Throughout the months of June, July and August I must have received a reminder letter from various people at least once a week. It turned out that we hadn't registered with the FA, hadn't registered with the league (and now faced a late-renewal fine), hadn't confirmed our pitch bookings and I had not been to the recent AGM. That would be the AGM that I knew absolutely nothing about. How was I supposed to get from work to Dartford to West London during the week for an AGM? I just ignored that one and have heard nothing on it since.

It was time to introduce myself to the squad, but even that seemed pretty thin on the ground. Over the last few years the likes of Rich Davis (moved down to Cornwall), Carlos Sanchez (moved to Spain), Sameer Joomun (moved to East London – worst excuse ever!), Hakan Duran (work commitments) and other not so regular players had all announced their unavailability, either completely or certainly for most games. I was left with about fifteen players, only six of which were week-in/week-out regulars.

Fortunately Pete and Step had introduced their two cousins, Nick and James, to the club during the previous season so it wasn't all bad. Then James announced that he was going travelling to Australia for a year! Early on in the season Ross also had to 'retire.' He got an injury which kept him out until Christmas and then got married and moved up to Northampton – sadly, both on a personal and football level, we have not seen or heard much from him since. Another two to cross off the list then...

Despite all my mockery and moaning, Omer had been a saviour for the club. Just as I was doing now, he had taken over from Des with little experience and had had to learn it the hard way. Of course he had his faults – what manager didn't? The key one was his tendency to write-off an opposition even before kickoff. If we were playing the team bottom of the league, you could be sure that an email would be on its way saying that he expected us to score at least five or six. In professional terms, it would be the same as Manchester United being drawn at home to Grimsby Town in the FA Cup and Sir Alex Ferguson coming out in his press conference and proudly stating "this lot are rubbish, we are going to thrash them." Instead, he keeps it sensible and polite and goes for something like "we know it isn't going to be easy but we need to make sure that we get the job done." Both basically mean the same thing, but one doesn't make you look quite so stupid if it all goes horribly wrong.

The first time this happened was against, the then hapless, Facile Tigre. Although we had in the region of twenty shots over the course of the game, we failed to hit the target once. They went up the other end, had one shot, scored and we lost one nil.

Perhaps the most high profile cock-up during Omer's reign came against SW2. We had played them earlier on in the season and beat them 3-2. The score line suggests that the game was close but it was far from it. It was one of the most one-sided and convincing one goal victories that you are ever likely to see. Therefore, when we were drawn against them in the semi-final of the Challenge Cup everybody was understandably confident. This was until we received 'the dreaded email.' Upon requesting player availability for the game, Omer described SW2 as, and I quote, "deliciously shite." It was a fantastic phrase to use and was entirely accurate, but wasn't necessarily appropriate. As you have probably guessed we lost the game, and lost it in style - four-nil to be exact. SW2 had indeed been "deliciously shite" but we had gone one step further and had been absolutely bloody dreadful!

My playing career on its own was now officially over. I had had five incredible years and it was now time for a new era to begin. A summary of those seasons can be found over the next few pages.

2004-2005 Season
West End (London) A.F.A. Sunday AM
First Division

		P	W	D	L	F	A	Pts
1	Inter Clapham	20	15	3	2	74	35	48
2	Hyde Athletic	20	13	4	3	58	31	43
3	Deportivo Atlas	20	13	2	5	50	30	41
4	**Nice Fridge**	**20**	**12**	**1**	**7**	**60**	**36**	**37**
5	AFC Clapham	20	10	1	9	51	49	31
6	Old Theonians	20	9	3	8	60	45	30
7	Churchill Arms	20	6	3	11	53	60	21
8	Inter Camden	20	7	0	13	55	65	21
9	Club KK FC	20	7	0	13	44	57	21
10	Hampstead SDA	20	5	2	13	48	93	17
11	Facile Tigre	20	3	1	16	32	84	10

Nice Fridge	1	vs	4	AFC Clapham
Churchill Arms	4	vs	2	Nice Fridge
Nice Fridge	2	vs	4	Hyde Athletic
Old Theonians	0	vs	3	Nice Fridge
Nice Fridge	5	vs	3	Facile Tigre
Nice Fridge	8	vs	1	Hampstead SDA
Nice Fridge	4	vs	1	Club KK FC
Deportivo Atlas	1	vs	5	Nice Fridge
Inter Camden	1	vs	5	Nice Fridge
Facile Tigre	2	vs	6	Nice Fridge
Inter Clapham	2	vs	1	Nice Fridge
Club KK FC	2	vs	6	Nice Fridge
AFC Clapham	1	vs	3	Nice Fridge
Hampstead SDA	3	vs	6	Nice Fridge
Nice Fridge	0	vs	2	Deportivo Atlas
Nice Fridge	2	vs	3	Inter Clapham
Nice Fridge	0	vs	0	Old Theonians
Hyde Athletic	2	vs	1	Nice Fridge
Nice Fridge	Home win awarded			Inter Camden
Nice Fridge	Home win awarded			Churchill Arms

2005-2006 Season
West End (London) A.F.A.
Sunday AM First Division

		P	W	D	L	F	A	Pts
1	Deportivo Atlas	22	15	3	4	64	22	48
2	AFC Clapham	22	15	3	4	63	33	48
3	**Nice Fridge**	**22**	**13**	**5**	**4**	**64**	**42**	**44**
4	Old Theonians	22	12	3	7	46	40	39
5	Churchill Arms	22	11	5	6	64	50	38
6	A Small World	22	10	3	9	56	40	33
7	Swaffham Exiles	22	9	2	11	42	54	29
8	Brixton Team X	22	8	4	10	59	62	28
9	Athletico Inter	22	9	1	12	48	62	28
10	Inter Camden	22	5	4	13	44	52	19
11	Facile Tigre	22	4	2	16	35	88	14
12	Hampstead SDA	22	2	3	17	47	87	9

Nice Fridge	4	vs	1	Churchill Arms
Nice Fridge	3	vs	3	Hampstead SDA
Old Theonians	1	vs	1	Nice Fridge
Nice Fridge	2	vs	0	Inter Camden
Brixton Team X	4	vs	5	Nice Fridge
Athletico Inter	3	vs	2	Nice Fridge
Facile Tigre	2	vs	7	Nice Fridge
Inter Camden	4	vs	0	Nice Fridge
Deportivo Atlas	0	vs	2	Nice Fridge
Nice Fridge	5	vs	1	A Small World
Nice Fridge	2	vs	1	Athletico Inter
Hampstead SDA	2	vs	4	Nice Fridge
Nice Fridge	4	vs	1	Swaffham Exiles
Nice Fridge	1	vs	2	AFC Clapham
Nice Fridge	1	vs	1	Old Theonians
Churchill Arms	4	vs	4	Nice Fridge
A Small World	5	vs	0	Nice Fridge
Nice Fridge	1	vs	0	Deportivo Atlas
Swaffham Exiles	2	vs	4	Nice Fridge
Nice Fridge	6	vs	3	Brixton Team X
Nice Fridge	1	vs	1	Facile Tigre
AFC Clapham	1	vs	5	Nice Fridge

2006-2007 Season
West End (London) A.F.A.
Sunday AM - Division One

		P	W	D	L	F	A	Pts
1	AFC Clapham	14	9	1	4	40	16	28
2	A Small World	14	6	5	3	29	23	23
3	Churchill Arms	14	7	1	6	37	31	22
4	Fat Cats	14	7	0	7	22	31	21
5	Swaffham Exiles	14	5	4	5	26	28	19
6	Facile Tigre	14	5	2	7	37	47	17
7	Old Theonians	14	4	3	7	25	34	15
8	**Nice Fridge**	**14**	**4**	**2**	**8**	**23**	**29**	**14**

Nice Fridge	3	vs	5	Facile Tigre
A Small World	2	vs	1	Nice Fridge
Nice Fridge	8	vs	0	Old Theonians
Nice Fridge	2	vs	5	Churchill Arms
Swaffham Exiles	0	vs	0	Nice Fridge
AFC Clapham	0	vs	1	Nice Fridge
Facile Tigre	2	vs	0	Nice Fridge
Nice Fridge	2	vs	3	A Small World
Churchill Arms	2	vs	3	Nice Fridge
Nice Fridge	0	vs	5	Swaffham Exiles
Nice Fridge	2	vs	4	AFC Clapham
Fat Cats	1	vs	0	Nice Fridge
Nice Fridge	1	vs	0	Fat Cats
Old Theonians	0	vs	0	Nice Fridge

2007-2008 Season

West End (London) A.F.A.
Sunday AM - Division One

		P	W	D	L	F	A	Pts
1	Ship (The)	14	10	0	4	58	27	30
2	FC Colossal	14	9	1	4	39	27	28
3	Swaffham Exiles	14	7	3	4	35	32	24
4	**Nice Fridge**	**14**	**6**	**5**	**3**	**34**	**25**	**23**
5	AFC Millbank	14	6	0	8	51	30	18
6	Fat Cats	14	4	6	4	34	35	18
7	Old Theonians	14	3	3	8	33	54	12
8	Facile Tigre	14	1	2	11	30	84	5

Old Theonians	3	vs	6	Nice Fridge
Nice Fridge	4	vs	1	The Ship
Fat Cats	1	vs	1	Nice Fridge
Nice Fridge	1	vs	1	Swaffham Exiles
Nice Fridge	0	vs	0	Fat Cats
Facile Tigre	1	vs	7	Nice Fridge
Swaffham Exiles	1	vs	3	Nice Fridge
Nice Fridge	2	vs	2	Old Theonians
FC Colossal	3	vs	2	Nice Fridge
Nice Fridge	3	vs	2	AFC Millbank
The Ship	4	vs	1	Nice Fridge
Nice Fridge	2	vs	2	Facile Tigre
AFC Millbank	4	vs	0	Nice Fridge
Nice Fridge	2	vs	0	FC Colossal

2008-2009 Season

West End (London) A.F.A.

Sunday AM - Division One

		P	W	D	L	F	A	Pts
1	AFC Millbank	18	12	5	1	62	19	41
2	Swaffham Exiles	18	10	5	3	57	35	35
3	**Nice Fridge**	**18**	**9**	**3**	**6**	**46**	**35**	**30**
4	SW2 FC	18	8	5	5	41	40	29
5	Facile Tigre	18	3	5	10	25	54	14
6	Fat Cats	18	3	4	11	29	49	13
7	Old Theonians	18	3	3	12	31	59	12

Old Theonians	2	vs	0	Nice Fridge
Fat Cats	1	vs	3	Nice Fridge
Nice Fridge	2	vs	5	AFC Millbank
Swaffham Exiles	3	vs	3	Nice Fridge
Nice Fridge	5	vs	1	Fat Cats
Nice Fridge	3	vs	2	SW2 FC
AFC Millbank	3	vs	1	Nice Fridge
Nice Fridge	2	vs	3	Swaffham Exiles
Fat Cats	1	vs	3	Nice Fridge
Facile Tigre	2	vs	1	Nice Fridge
Swaffham Exiles	6	vs	2	Nice Fridge
AFC Millbank	2	vs	2	Nice Fridge
Nice Fridge	4	vs	0	Old Theonians
Old Theonians	1	vs	7	Nice Fridge
Nice Fridge	1	vs	1	SW2 FC
SW2 FC	1	vs	2	Nice Fridge
Nice Fridge	3	vs	1	Facile Tigre
Nice Fridge	2	vs	0	Facile Tigre

Hyde & Seek

It all unofficially began on Sunday 30th August 2009. I had arranged a pre-season friendly against Facile Tigre. I figured that it would not only be a good game for me to get into the swing of things, but also ideal for the players who had not had a competitive game in over three months. One of the key points that Omer had used to sell this management idea to me was that I would never be short of players – apparently everyone always helped out and if you were ever short then somebody else would change their plans to make up the numbers.

It turned out that this wasn't entirely true. At first everything went according to plan. My first email immediately got eleven definite replies, which, considering it was a summer friendly over the August Bank Holiday, wasn't a bad effort at all. By Saturday night it had shrunk to a measly seven with four poor sods having to admit defeat that the missus had "better ideas" on ways to spend the weekend. I'd imagine that Bluewater, Westfields or the local garden centre are wonderful places to go!

A desperate text followed with Shogo replying that he had a mate who would be able to come along and play. Until this point Shogo Hirata had held the record for the shortest player in Nice Fridge history but, by all accounts, Jermaine (his mate) would come straight in at number one. That was until Jermaine did not show up. Apparently he had not played football in five years and therefore didn't have any football boots or shin pads – perhaps it was a blessing that he couldn't make it!

Fortunately for us (well, for me) Facile Tigre had also struggled for players and had only been able to get a grand total of eight. Another bit of good fortune came our way when we realised that we were going to be playing on the all-weather pitch at Hurlingham that is no more than three-quarter size of a normal football pitch.

As is always the case when you play football in local parks, you have to be prepared to be a bit forceful and politely ask the people that are already on it to "sling their hooks!" I left this to the Facile Tigre manager to worry about – after all, it was effectively their home game. The next stage that regularly follows is for these randoms to ask if they can join in. In their eyes it is a win-win situation for everybody, but that isn't strictly true as whether we said yes or no our game would still be going ahead. My immediate reaction was to tell them to get lost – this was a serious game between two properly affiliated sides and didn't need three unknown 'locals' jumping on board and ruining it for everybody. The fact that all three were allowed to play goes some way to show how much influence and power I had on the situation really! Facile Tigre chose a tall centre-half called Paul and we were left with two stocky guys that went by the names of Abs and Tony.

There is nothing of note to mention on the game to be honest. It was one of the hottest days of the year and was an eight-on-eight kick around – there really wasn't going to be anything incredible to report. We did actually win the game 4-1, with the random Tony scoring two from close range. At the time I didn't make much of that, but looking back I probably should have been concerned that the match winner for Nice Fridge was a bloke who we had all met just some ninety minutes earlier.

As both sides were getting changed after the game various conversations started up – some to do with the summer, some family related and some your typical random male footballer chit-chat. It then turned to something completely different. Out of nowhere, the Facile Tigre player-manager asked Abs, Tony and Paul if they played for a club. It turned out that they didn't and that they would love to wear the fluorescent orange of the Tigre's for the forthcoming season. Was this the way that Sunday league management worked these days? Find some people that look like they have once played football and commit yourself to picking them for at least the next eight months – I was taking notes!

A few days later I received a much unexpected email from an Anthony Bunce. It took me a while to realise who this was, but then it clicked. The clue was in the email really:

"Hi mate, it's Tony who played with Abs and Paul in your game against Facile Tigre the other day."

There would have been some serious issues if I had still been unsure as to who it was from. It turned out that they were no longer going to be playing for Facile Tigre, which raised two immediate questions – firstly, what had happened or been said that meant the 'triple-deal' had fallen through and secondly, how the hell had he got my email address?

The email went on to ask if we were in need of any players. I'm sure that he must have written it fairly sarcastically – after all, he had seen the shambles of the game that had lead to this situation! My immediate reaction was to make up some elaborate excuse, in order to get him off my case. Call me selective but I had set my heights and standards slightly higher than signing Facile Tigre rejects. That wasn't the direction that I had envisaged the club to be going in.

Despite these thoughts, I found myself typing a reply that starting along the lines of "sure we would love to have you on board – the more the merrier." Some may argue that I was being incredibly two-faced but I did have a couple of very good reasons. The first is that I do not have the ability to say no. It is just something that has affected me all my life – I simply don't like upsetting people. Before any of the team get any ideas, no you can't go on a pay-as-you-play contract, you most definitely cannot play upfront (strikers excluded, obviously) and yes, you do still have to pay your subs for the season. I also extend this to cover any other trick questions that may arise throughout my managerial career.

The other reason that I agreed to take Tony, Abs and Paul onboard was the final line of his email. Why they did not feel the need to mention this at the game on Sunday, I do not know but Tony announced that they used to play for Hyde Athletic. Those of you that paid any attention to the previous league tables will know that they were promoted from Division One back in 2005 – if you did not know this then you should be ashamed of yourselves! In the following seasons Hyde held their own in the top division and even went onto win the league one year. Unfortunately for them, due to various circumstances, the team folded and all three had been without a club ever since. I was in the same situation a professional manager may have been in if he were given three players from Torquay, only to find out that they had previously played for Real Madrid – you may have to use your imagination slightly there!

To be honest, I didn't really expect them to have much of an influence on the side. I imagined that they would all play the first few games and then start making some excuses for unavailability and that we would never see them again. In their defence, they were the complete opposite. Between the three of them they only missed one game all season.

Moving on with pre-season, we had one more friendly to get ourselves motivated and prepared for the eight months that were ahead of us. It was against our long-term friends, Old Theonians – a side that have always been notoriously average. With that in mind, I came away from the game with two thoughts in the head. By the way, we lost 5-1 and this is what sent my brain into over-drive. Either they had become amazing in the space of six months, or we had become absolutely rubbish. Whichever it was, it certainly wasn't ideal.

Onwards and upwards and all that – my first managerial season was upon us and our opening fixture was somewhat of an unknown. It was against a brand new team called The Masons Arms (I assume they are pub related in some way) which meant that they would hopefully take a while to settle down and gel together. The best thing that we could do was hit them hard from the start. My pre-match team talk was already sorted.

While arranging everything with the opposition manager he dropped into the conversation that "most of the team" were going to be at a wedding the night before and therefore he did not know what state they would turn up in. I decided that it would be best if I didn't break this news to the team – I had seen the effects that Omer's comments had had in the past! By the time we were all ready to kick-off no fewer than eight of our team had been told the news. I would love to blame somebody else but it was entirely my fault. First of all I told Step and Pete, which meant it then came up in conversation in the car (and McDonalds) so Chris, Ross and Nick knew. I then convinced myself that Matty (the captain) and Omer (ex-manager) needed to know, which finally extended to Neil who I was keen to use to help me with my tactics and team-talks etc. In hindsight, it probably would have been easier to just put it in an email and get it out in the open. This management malarkey was hard work and the game hadn't even kicked off yet!

Look At The Lions

The game kicked off at 10:30am on Sunday 13th August 2009. By 10:50am on that same Sunday 13th August 2009 we found ourselves losing 2-0. It's not as if we were bad, they were just very, very good. For a team that had apparently never played together before and were supposed to still be drunk they passed the ball around with great confidence and picked their passes one by one. They didn't panic, they didn't rush and they were incredibly composed, but when they needed to get physical they had that option as well. Their main threat came from a striker who is a spitting image of Emmanuel Adebayor – he had the same build, same height, same hair and even same facial hair. In fact, we should have probably asked for some proof to show that it wasn't the 'real' Adebayor.

The game itself was being played at Regents Park and it is fair to say that Nice Fridge, both since and before the merger, do not have a good record there. Fortunately we do not play there very often but in the past we had convincingly lost 3-1, 4-0 and 2-0. It is definitely not somewhere that I have particularly fond memories of! As a venue and set-up it is comfortably the best in the league. The changing rooms are in the centre of the park and these are only a few years old, following what must have been a fairly substantial grant from the Lottery Fund. Each of the rooms, of which there must be at least twenty, have working (and clean) showers, as well as mirrors and hairdryers for the Cristiano's of this World. Saying that, we have seen the likes of Watford and Spurs Ladies playing there so that could go someway to explaining that. At the top of 'The Hub' (that is it's real name and not some affectionate nickname I have given it) there is a café that gives uninterrupted views of all of the pitches, with fully functioning heating and lighting.

For those that do not know their London geography Regents Park runs alongside London Zoo, with just a single fence separating the two, very different, venues. On a recent visit to the Zoo I was more impressed that I could see the matches being played than the animals that I was supposed to be there for. I even considered jumping over the fence to go and sit on the touchline, but then I would have effectively paid thirty quid to watch an amateur football match between two unknown sides. There is probably more to gain if you jump the fence in the opposite direction – not that I am condoning that sort of behaviour, you must understand. When standing in goal on certain pitches at Regents Park you can actually see some of the lions and the entrance to the penguin enclosure, which is quite a strange experience when you think about it. Looking back, my fascination with these lions could have something to do with the fact that I had conceded nine goals in just three games at the Park.

During our heaviest defeat at Regents Park, Pete and I actually had an argument that stretched the length of the pitch. He wanted me to take a quick goal-kick as they were short at the back, but I decided to hold onto the ball as he was the only one of our players forward and I didn't think he would have the strength to beat their centre-back. Comments went back and forth for the next five minutes or so, until Rich told us both, in no uncertain terms, to shut up! Baring in mind that we have known each other from the age of eight it really had been unexpected and I must admit that I did seriously consider my playing career at this stage. Not because of a childish argument, but because I didn't want something like this to come between a long-term friendship again.

For once, we had a fairly decent turn out of spectators on the touchline. The most notable was Ian Sharp – Step and Pete's dad for those that have forgotten. Ian has an incredible knowledge of football and I reckon would be an absolute star if it came to a football quiz. You can be sure that wherever Ian is on the touchline, the camera will not be far away. What is even more impressive is that he seems to have a psychic brain when it comes to knowing what is going to follow. You can guarantee that he will capture every goal, every highlight and usually every lowlight – certainly where I am concerned anyway.

I do, however, have a few criticisms of him - the first being that he is a Wolverhampton Wanderers fan. Now I have nothing against Wolves at all, but it doesn't seem like the sort of club that you would support unless you actually lived in Birmingham and even then, I would be tempted to put Aston Villa on the top of the list. So, where does he live then, I hear you ask?

Bristol... Yes, as in the city just over the water from Wales that has two of its own teams to choose from.

On top of that, he has also made the big mistake of marrying a Tottenham Hotspur fan. You have probably already got a rough idea of my opinion on that North London club so I won't take it any further. Suffice to say though, his extensive football brain has clearly had an impact on his decision making.

Back to the game and we were slowly making our presence known to The Masons Arms. We had calmed down from the early double setback and were now starting to create a few chances of our own. We had spotted that they were relatively weak down the wings and wanted to exploit this as much as possible. It didn't take long for the plan to reap its rewards. A cross came into the box and Shogo (remember he is still officially the shortest player in the club's history) leapt like a salmon to get onto the end of it. From nowhere, the ball came off his head like a bullet and flew into the top left hand corner and we had halved the deficit with a potential goal of the season. Obviously, at the time, it was the goal of the season. Consequently, Shogo is now the proud owner of the record for the shortest player to ever score a header for Nice Fridge Locomotiv Football Club. Surely an MBE is just round the corner?

In perfect Nice Fridge fashion we were keen to let this lead slip and they soon had their two goal cushion back. Clearly it did not matter who the manager was, it was simply something that all Nice Fridge teams were good at! Half time came and I chose this opportunity to tell the wedding story to the few players that were not already in the know and it worked an absolute treat. Everybody was fired up again – they were expecting The Masons Arms to get worn out towards the end and saw that this game was anything but over. Within fifteens minutes of the second half we had pulled it back to 3-3, thanks to Omer and Pete. The came the moment of my season...

They were awarded a free-kick on the edge of the box, so I arranged my wall with the help of Pete, as we did for any other set piece around the penalty area. The ball curled up and over the wall and I dived to my right to make a decent, but fairly routine, save. As I landed on my right side, I heard a loud crunch and felt a sudden pain. In absolute agony (and true Iker Casillas style) all I could do was parry the ball back into play and towards the feet of their onrushing striker. I rose to my feet as quick as possible and threw myself at the feet of their player. I had judged it perfectly and held onto the ball tighter than ever before.

I had never been in this much pain before and immediately tried to throw the ball out of play with the hope of getting some medical attention. I had no option but to go off the field, with Pete going in goal as my replacement. The problem was that we had already made our three substitutions so we were down to ten men. After five minutes of trying everything to loosen my shoulder, I had to admit defeat – there was no way that I would be able to go back in goal.

The Masons Arms had, by now, sensed that this could be their chance to get a late winner and were pushing more and more men forward. The least I could do was to go back onto the field as an outfield player, even if it was to just make up the numbers. I think I am being generous to myself there, as I was absolutely useless. I couldn't run without having to hold my arm, couldn't jump, couldn't turn and certainly didn't have any intention of going in for any tackles. I was quite literally a waste of space.

Unfortunately they did go on to get a late winner and take the game 4-3. We were certainly disappointed but you could see that everybody was already acting as one team. We had no repeat of the Locomotiv-merger friendly and were consoling one another all the way back to the changing rooms.

It turned out that the first dive had dislocated my right shoulder and the second had put it back in place. The only problem with it going back into its socket was that it twisted my collarbone and tore the ligament at the same time – no wonder that it bloody hurt so much!

I didn't realise this at the time, but that injury effectively ended my season. Between then and the last game of the season on 9th May, I would only feature in another five and even they were played through the pain barrier. It was going to be a long old campaign!

Bloody Egg-Chasers

Following that opening day defeat we went on an amazing run. Out of the next five games we picked up a total of zero points – not one; zilch; nothing. The commitment and passion were certainly there but we just couldn't seem to gel. Perhaps the biggest problem was the fact that we had to put Pete in goal. Don't get me wrong, Pete is a very good goalkeeper and certainly wasn't responsible for any of the goals that he conceded during his time between the sticks, but we simply missed his pace and finishing upfront.

As you have read by now, our long time get-out clause had been the long ball up to the striker for him to chase onto and put the defence under pressure. No disrespect here to Tony and Omer but neither of them are blessed with pace, which meant that as quick as we were clearing the ball it was coming straight back at us.

On the back of these results I bet Tony, Abs and Paul were regretting their decision to not stay with Facile Tigre, who, in comparison to us at the time, must have seemed world class. In the first four games we had scored an impressive twelve goals, but conceded an even more impressive twenty. We lost 8-4 in one of the worst performances I have ever witnessed and then followed that up with a 5-2 defeat to Fernhead Rovers. Incidentally, that was one of only two games that they won all season, which says a lot for how we were playing really. The next game finished in a 3-3 draw, but it was a cup game (the Challenge Trophy, not 'our cup' don't panic) and we subsequently lost on penalties. I'm classing that as a defeat but if Jose Mourinho is to be believed, apparently that does not count. Don't forget, he is the Special One!

By the end of this season we actually used a total of eight different goalkeepers. Pete, Step, Neil (all three in the defeat to Fernhead), Adam, Tony, Paul (Tony's mate, not the Paul that you know of), Omer and myself all wore the legendary Number One jersey at some stage. Now, I don't mean to be big-headed here but our opening win of the season came in my first game back after my injury. Originally, I had no intention of playing but just as Ross and I had joined the A2 to start the usual long journey, I received a text message from Omer giving some excuse about how his wife had cut her hand open the night before and he therefore could not play. I had no option but to go back and get my kit, despite still being injured.

      I decided to keep my warm-up to a minimum. Some may say that I should have made it more thorough than normal, but I had such low confidence of it getting through the full ninety minutes I wanted to put as little strain on it as possible. The game was against Facile Tigre and we convincingly won 4-1, with Pete getting two and yours truly saving a penalty. This game on its own proved that trying to swap me and Pete round, position-wise, wasn't going to work as a long-term solution. Not that we didn't know that already.

      And then it happened again. The game against Barnet Eagles came just a few weeks later and I was starting to get a bit more optimistic with my progress - forget the team for the time being, my main aim was to be able to move my arm in a full circle. I slid out at the same time as their striker came charging in and parried the ball away to safety – that on its own is a rarity for more, as I am definitely not renowned for my bravery. A few seconds later I learnt why I had been right to bottle challenges in the past. Their striker, weighing easily in excess of eighteen stone, continued to fall towards me and landed directly on my right shoulder. I don't think the fact that I was already suffering from an injury made any difference at all, but my shoulder had nowhere to go other than pop out again. With the size of the guy that had collapsed on me, I'm surprised that my arm didn't just completely disconnect itself from my body and run away - I would have done if I had known a few seconds earlier. As I trudged off the pitch again, their captain decided that now would be a good time to tell me that their striker usually played rugby. What did he really want me to do with that sort of useless information? All it meant was rather than walking off dejected, I left the field of play mumbling obscenities to myself about "bloody peanut-huggers and egg-chasers."

      Another visit to the hospital meant that I was now diagnosed with Calcification in my shoulder. Apparently it means that fragments of my bone had broken away and that the body was trying to 'repair' it by forming a barrier. In turn, this is what causes the pain. Why can't the body just mind its own business? Following a number of X-Rays and MRI scans I was advised that it would hopefully heal itself over time, otherwise I would have no option but to have an operation.

You are not to know this, but I have never had much luck when it comes to injuries. Don't get me wrong, I haven't never really suffered anything serious and fortunately have not yet broken a bone but I tend to go for the obscure ones – both in terms of what the injury is and also how it actually happens.

Whilst at secondary school I managed to get head butted and knocked out during a session of touch rugby (see above for my thoughts on 'that' sport) and then missed two years of sport because I grew too quickly. Yes, you read that correct – I shot up in height so fast that my knee muscles could not keep up, meaning that my knee caps both pointed outwards at a ridiculously awkward angle instead of being straight, like evolution intended them to be.

Then there is the previously mentioned collision with Colin, a bout of shin splints that came out of nowhere, a pulled muscle in the bottom of my back and a torn thumb ligament in my right hand that was caused by falling over whilst playing in a ten-pin bowling league.

At primary school I even managed to knock myself out by standing up quickly in the cloakroom and smashing my head against the underside of a coat hook! Perhaps the most random came in the summer of 2010 when I was diagnosed with Pericarditis – an unusual illness that results in the heart membrane swelling up and suffocating the heart. It feels like a heart attack but isn't so serious. I was kept in hospital for a few days and it subsequently took a good few months to even get close to full fitness again.

As a club we have certainly been on the receiving end of a few serious injuries as well. Before a 'proper' warm-up was introduced the traditional pulled calf, hamstring and groin muscles were a weekly occurrence and still are if your name is Omer Kutluoglu but we have often taken things to the next level.

In consecutive games of my first season Andy Nuttall and Steven Reid both suffered serious head injuries that resulted in concussion and blood pouring everywhere. More amazingly, in both cases they tried to get up and carry on with the game – they just don't make centre backs like that anymore, do they? We have had a number of broken bones over the years, the most notable happening to a hapless Ross (not Jenner, another one who only played a few games) who managed to snap his shin and ankle in three places when going in for a fifty-fifty challenge. The tackle took place on the edge of the opposition penalty area but the impact was so heavy that I heard it as clear as anything up the other end of the pitch. The other broken bone belongs to Step who somehow managed to break his metatarsal by jogging for a ball. There was nobody within five metres of him and he just suddenly pulled up – it was at the time when metatarsal injuries were all the rage so he may have just wanted some attention.

  We were reasonably fortunate during the 2009/2010 season. There were once again plenty of muscle complaints and once again most of these came from Omer but Matty must take the plaudits for injury of the season. During that depressing game against Fernhead Rovers he slid for the ball near the touchline and landed awkwardly on his right hand. That seemed to be the end of the problem until he came over to show everyone that his finger was in fact at right angles to how it should be. Luckily it was only dislocated, but the sight was certainly an impressive one.

  Despite all of this, the best injury that I have ever had the 'privilege' of seeing actually happened on an opposition player. A high ball was played towards their left wing where Chris was faced with one of their midfielders charging towards him. By the time the ball actually got to Chris's foot (or should I say by the time Chris' foot got the ball) their player couldn't have been more than two yards away. In typical Chris style he put his full bodyweight into the clearance and caught their midfielder square in the face. He fell to the ground as if he had been shot and twenty one other players followed him onto the ground, except we were all in fits of laughter. By sheer luck Carlos was recording this passage of play on his mobile phone and it has since done the rounds on at least ten different memory cards. I am pleased to say that the guy was not injured as such, but he was substituted quickly after – apparently not being able to walk in a straight line or remembering your teammates name is not normal. They should see Jez on a Sunday morning!

From a personal point of view, my management dream was very much coming true just not in the way that I had originally planned. At the start of the season my concerns had been how I would cope with running a side at the same time as concentrating on my own game, but my body had been kind enough to come up with a solution for me. I must admit that I was really enjoying it, although it was a lot harder and more stressful than I ever imagined it to be. To be honest, if we had had a permanent replacement for me in goal I may well have considered hanging up my boots for a while and just stuck with the management side of things.

Deep down, the results were not actually bothering me too much. Yes, it was disappointing and frustrating to not be winning but I was getting more enjoyment from the responsibilities and pressures that came with the role. The thing that I found the hardest was keeping it fair for everybody. It's all well and good selecting a team to go out and win but you also have to take into consideration the fact that these individuals are giving up their Sunday morning and you cannot expect the same people to sit on the bench every week. There are probably three or four players who I wouldn't consider subbing but I have to work out the best way to give everybody else the same amount of game time. Fortunately I have an incredible group of players, the majority of whom do not take it personally if I take them off or start them sub and know that it will equal itself out. And for that I am very grateful!

What A Friendly Bunch

The winter of 2009/10 will be remembered across the whole country for the effect that the snow had on everybody. Whether it be problems getting to work or postponements of sporting events at all levels, nobody was able to escape it. If the Premier League grounds were unable to cope, what chance did the local parks around London have?

From 30th November 2009 all the way through to 13th February 2010 we only had two games that went ahead – it was going to be a long second half of the season. In terms of my rehabilitation, the snow was definitely working in my favour. I was making good progress and luckily enough didn't have the peer-pressure from others and myself to make an early return. All of them plans soon went out of the window though when I suffered a car crash on my way to work. Nothing serious fortunately, but it did dislocate my right shoulder again and also had an impact on my left. It turned out that I was back to the drawing board in terms of my recovery, but I did at least get some private physiotherapy out of it, so it is all swings and roundabouts I suppose.

By now the team were used to not having a permanent goalkeeper. But what we lacked in this department was more than made up for with our centre back partnership. Paul Burnham had made the position his own and had been joined by Adam Bunce (Tony's brother) who had both played together in the Hyde Athletic days so knew each others strengths and weaknesses. They were as solid as any other combination you will see on a Sunday morning, whether that be through excellent defending or cynical tackling – at this level, they all count. We were slowly picking up results and also beginning to play well, two things that came together perfectly on 14th March against Fat Cats.

It had been another difficult week in terms of numbers, with only ten regulars announcing their availability. For once it wasn't Jez doing the dropping out, instead he managed to get hold of a friend, Kevin, who was able to play.

As kick-off approached we only appeared to have nine men - both Kevin and Shogo were missing and nobody could get hold of them. Eventually they did both appear, Shogo gave himself a full two minutes to get ready and Kevin left it even later with only thirty seconds to spare. In fact, I think the game actually kicked off before Kevin was fully changed and ready to start.

Within the first five minutes Kevin had pulled his groin muscle and Nick had twisted his ankle by falling down a rabbit hole (one of the extra challenges that come with Sunday league football) in his customary left back position. To their credit, both battled on heroically, as did Matty, Jez and Tony who also picked up first half muscle injuries. We were effectively down to six fully fit players but you wouldn't have known it if you were watching the game as an outsider. We were winning every tackle, covering every blade of grass and working for one another like never before.

The game was incredible but it did have a couple of sour points. The first was another injury to our captain Matty Russell. He had battled through the pain barrier in the first half, but stretched for one ball too many as the half time whistle approached and simply could not carry on. Unfortunately for him (and us) that would pretty much be the end of his season - with him going off injured twice more in the final months of the campaign. Any team in the league would miss a midfielder and captain to the standard of Matty – it is the same as Liverpool trying to cope without Steven Gerrard or Arsenal lining up without Cesc Fabregas (the latter is still valid at the time of going to press).

I should point out that Ian Sharp was once again present at the game and yes, he did have his camera with him. I don't know how he does it, but he certainly has the knack of picking what games to come and watch. I put it all down to his over-sized football brain.

As I said before, the whole team were working together as a unit but this is where the second sour point comes in. For some unknown reason Abs decided to take it upon himself to rearrange the body features of the Fat Cats striker. Quite literally out of nowhere, he launched himself on the back of the unsuspecting forward and dragged him to the ground. It doesn't take a genius to work out that the ref produced a red card, even though Abs did find the time to protest his innocence. I still have no idea what happened to cause the reaction, but would love to know what excuse he tried to use when attempting to get out of the sending off. I'm not sure the best lawyer in the world would have been able to overturn that decision!

So, with Matty off the field injured and Vinnie Jones, sorry Abs, sent off we were down to nine men. Fortunately we were already three-nil up at this point so did have some flexibility with our plans. It was quite a simple management decision really – defend!

Despite not being on the field of play, I would like to think that both Abs and myself had a positive impact on the final result. Every time the ball went out of play for our goal kick we took it in turns to go and collect the ball on Tony's (he was the stand-in 'keeper this week) behalf. I appreciate this does not sound much but over the years I have mastered the art of the famous 'goalkeeper jog.' In simple terms, you look as if you are running to get the ball but are actually going no faster than you would be if you were walking – for the advanced members, it is possible to end up going slower than a walk. This wastes valuable minutes every single time and there is nothing the ref can do about it. He couldn't say anything to Abs as he had already sent him off and wasn't going to say anything to me as it looked like I was doing everybody a favour by trying to keep the game flowing. Saying that, even if I had been the goalkeeper playing and gone to get the ball, the ref still wouldn't have said anything – you just don't get booked for time wasting in Sunday league football. If I was playing in the Premier League I would have more yellow cards to my name than Jens Lehmann managed to pick up in his whole career.

Another technique that has a similar outcome is the accidental mis-placed pass. As the goalkeeper, you summon somebody else to fetch the ball for you. As they are running past make sure you tell them which side of the goal you will be standing on and ensure that they proceed to pass the ball to the very opposite. It comes from experience as to how much of an over-weighted pass you can get away with, but even if it only happens once it is still another thirty seconds off of the clock. If you can initiate both of these techniques in one go, then I bow down to you. You can certainly join me in the elite club!

The game eventually finished 4-1 and fortunately we had three weeks for all of the walking (and some not walking anymore) wounded to recover in time for our next game.

There are very few things that haven't happened at some stage during Nice Fridge's history but Sunday 11th April 2010 will always go down in the memory banks as a famous first. It had been talked about since pre-season but had now finally been arranged. It was time for Nice Fridge Locomotiv vs Nice Fridge Veterans.

The match report can be read in all its glory later on, but suffice to say it was an absolute epic. I had managed to do some bartering before kick-off with Gruber who was managing The Veterans. He wanted to bring in a couple of younger faces to ensure that they kept going for the full ninety minutes (I like to refer to them as 'ringers'), so I decided that this would be acceptable as long as I got my side of the bargain as well – that they had Jez and Omer. I'd been waiting all season to be able to drop them from the side (not for anything performance related, but simply because I could) and, trust me, it felt good.

The game was played in very high spirits, with the likes of Colin Gibson, Seb White, Martinez, Pasco, David Carr and Nawaz all making appearances. As far as the 'new' half of Nice Fridge Locomotiv were concerned this was just another game of football against a slightly (very) aging side but for the likes of Step, Pete, Chris and myself this was an emotional and special game that needed to be treated with the respect it deserved.

Just a few weeks later I received a rather unexpected phone call from Rik, the WELAFA league secretary to confirm the plans and arrangements for the Sportsmanship Shield Field on 9th May. I'm not going to lie to you, I had absolutely no idea what he was talking about, but it sounded positive so I let him carry on. He ended by saying that he would put everything in an email which was very lucky indeed.

The email made a lot more sense and explained exactly why I didn't know what he was talking about – because nobody would have known what he was talking about. To cut a long story short, the terrible winter weather had obviously pushed back a fair amount of fixtures. The cup finals had been scheduled to take place on the weekend in question with the semi-finals the week before. However, these had also been postponed due to waterlogged pitches. Therefore, as the venue had already been booked and paid for they had decided to bring back an old competition to take its place. The one-off game for the Sportsmanship Shield between two teams that regularly played the game in the right spirit – clearly the ref hadn't reported Abs' red card against Fat Cats, for which we are now very grateful. I decided not to tell anybody the real story as to how we had ended up in a Cup Final and went for the rather elaborate excuse of citing the Respect Campaign and such like.

For some reason the date seemed familiar to me. It was only when I emailed the team that I realised that it was the same weekend as Chris's stag-do in Bristol. Chris (obviously), Step, Pete, Nick and myself would all be there, although I had arranged to come home on the Saturday instead of staying overnight like all of the others. Understandably, Chris immediately ruled himself out and Step agreed that he would also stay in Bristol. Pete and Nick, on the other hand, were very quick to confirm their attendance and would apparently do whatever it took to get back in time.

It was soon arranged that Chris, Step and Pete (as well as other non-Fridgers) would travel to Bristol on the Friday night and would be joined by Nick and myself Saturday morning in time for paintballing and go-karting. Nick would then stay with them in the hotel on Saturday night and I would return home to 'prepare' for the big game. Pete and Nick would then leave Bristol early on Sunday morning to get back to London in time for kick-off. Easy… yeah right!

London To Glasgow (And Back)

Apart from Nick managing to get my bank card (and only form of money) swallowed by a cash machine on the way to Bristol, the whole weekend went according to plan. Everybody stuck to their word and met at the ground at approximately 9:45am. What had I been worrying about? On paper it sounds so simple, but that is not really the full story. It doesn't take a genius to work out that Bristol is a fair distance from London and even further from Dartford. In order for this to all come together, a number of journeys had been needed.

For starters, Pete had driven his car to Bristol on the Friday night and I had done the same route Saturday morning. I then returned back home and drove to the ground in London on Sunday morning, the same time that Pete and Nick went from Bristol to London. Other than the final drive back home to Dartford you would think that is where the travelling ended, but there was a lot more. Pete had woken up on the Sunday morning feeling somewhat worse for wear and was in no fit state to drive, so arranged to jump in with this dad (yes, Ian was coming again) and leave his car in Bristol. This meant that after the game he had to go back to Bristol with his dad and then finally complete the weekend with the drive back to Dartford.

In total, for just three of the squad to be available for the game we had travelled almost 850 miles in under forty-eight hours. To put that distance into context, it is the same as driving from London to Glasgow and then just turning round and coming home again. It certainly wasn't good for our carbon footprint or the environment but I am sure that the powers-that-be would fully understand if we explained to them we were representing Nice Fridge Locomotiv in a Cup Final at Hanwell Town. Surely that excuse would allow you to get away with murder?

The final was set to be an absolute classic, especially with Ian in the terraces - he wouldn't have come if it wasn't going to be enjoyable. The game was against AFC Millbank who we have a very good relationship with. They are a decent bunch of lads and also a very good football team, playing the game in the right spirit without sacrificing the will to win.

As a team they are significantly stronger than us, with a couple of players that could run rings around most defences in the Premier Division. It, therefore, made sense for the game to be played at Hanwell Town – on our last visit we had defended throughout and caught Deportivo on the counter-attack and we would be setting out to do exactly the same today. As I entered the field of play and took up my position in goal, I realised just how close the terraces behind actually were. Fortunately the stands were basically empty but I could imagine just how intimidating it could be for an opposition goalkeeper if you had a few hundred fans throwing abuse at you for the full ninety minutes. It's all well and good saying that it must be awful having 40,000 people shouting at you during a Premiership game but at least they are in seats and are often quite a distance away. The only thing separating a non-league goalkeeper from an irate (and usually idiotic) fan is a three foot advertising hoarding that could be cleared in a second.

I'll let you savour the glory of the game in the match report on the following pages, but needless to say the scenes at the end were out of this world and the mood was euphoric.

On a personal level, my performance was one of the best in my Nice Fridge career. I made a close-range reaction save by tipping the ball over the bar that was actually described as "world class" (thanks Neil), a one-on-one save at the far post and an incredible 'I-knew-nothing-about-it-but-am-taking-all-the-credit-for-it' save in the second half. From how Nick has since described it to me, the cross came in from their left wing and was flicked on by their striker straight into my chest. It then ricocheted onto Nick's leg, back against my knee and was eventually cleared away. It was, without doubt, a case of being in the right place at the right time.

During the presentation ceremony Matty and I agreed to lift the shield together. The pictures of the manager and captain holding the shield aloft are enough to bring any grown man to tears – although I do have another ridiculous facial expression!

Once changed, we all headed to the bar to celebrate our victory and it was then that I decided to break the news to everybody as to the real reason we had 'qualified' for this cup final. None of the team was that surprised by the truth and even questioned whether I could have thought of a better excuse considering that Abs had been sent off the month before and we had had no fewer than three yellow cards throughout the season.

The subject was quickly changed when we were given our first bad news of the day. We were not going to be allowed to take the trophy home with us as the league wanted to get it engraved and have it presented to us at the AGM in June. This would normally have not been a problem but we had our own AGM in two weeks time and it would have been perfect to have the shield proudly standing on the head table. We even tried to arrange it so we could take it and then get it delivered straight to the engravers the Monday after our event, but they simply weren't changing their stance. They concluded that we couldn't be trusted with the responsibility and that if they had said yes to us then that would set a precedent for all of the other teams to do the same thing.

Couldn't trust us? How could they possibly say that? We were a team full of lawyers and solicitors… and it was at this very point that it hit home. We were no longer that team at all – we now consisted of engineers, salesmen, bailiffs and estate agents. It wasn't until that very conversation that I had realised how much of a transition we had been through. In the space of five years we had basically changed our entire squad, with the only remaining members being Omer, Jez and myself.

The faces may have been different but one thing was still the same - the Nice Fridge passion and commitment was as strong as ever. It is amazing what the famous shirt does to people. Somehow it manages to turn an average person into a star and if you are lucky enough to already be at star level, you immediately get elevated to legendary status. It really wouldn't surprise me if Lionel Messi announced that he had started his career with Nice Fridge, although you must understand that he would have had to have done his fair share of substitute appearances as well.

My first season in charge was officially over. It had been hard work, fun, stressful, enjoyable and, in the end, successful. The following pages of selected match reports from the season will give you an insight into the trials and tribulations that come with managing and playing in a Sunday league football team. And I wouldn't change it for the world!

Match Reports – Season 2009/10

Date : **Sunday 20th September 2009**
Venue : **Wormwood Scrubs**
Competition : **WELAFA Division One**

Nice Fridge Locomotiv   4   vs   8   Barnet Eagles
Pete Sharp
Omer Kutluoglu
Tony Bunce
Matty Russell (pen)

I think it is fair to say that was probably the worst ever performance by a Nice Fridge team. I'm not going to spend too much time on the game itself (after all, the sooner we forget about it the better I would say!).

For those of you not there, we started OK and took the lead midway through the first half - a good finish by Pete following a pretty good move all round. Then it all went a bit wrong... For the rest of the half we decided that there would be no need to put in any tackles, lost every single 50/50, lost most of the 80/20 tackles that should have been in our favour and went in at half time 5-1 (yes, five!) down...

Taking off Jez and Shogo at half time (no disrespect intended here to Shogo, every disrespect aimed at Jez!) seemed to work and we finally started to get stuck in. We were now winning the tackles, wanting to get hold of the ball and working for one another. Soon enough, we had pulled it back to 5-4 (thanks to good finishes from Omer and Tony and a well taken penalty from Matty). Our defensive generosity then reappeared and we proceeded to concede another three and the game finished 8-4 (Enough said, let's move on). Just quickly, can I give a special mention to Adam (Tony's brother). He was thrown in goal for his first game and despite conceding eight, certainly cannot be held responsible for any of the goals and in fact even made a number of decent saves to keep the score in single figures!

One thing this team has always been built on is teamwork and enjoyment. We have never been a superb footballing side (and I hasten to add, probably never will be!) but we have always got stuck in, always worked for one another and most importantly NEVER GIVEN UP!

We have already scored seven goals this season and should be sitting at the top of the league feeling very pleased for ourselves. However, we find ourselves at the other end, feeling very dejected!! There is no point people moaning at one another on the pitch - it's going to achieve nothing! Nobody means to make a mistake and everybody wants to do their best for the team. If somebody does make a mistake, we move on, support each other and make sure it doesn't happen again. AS A TEAM!

Date : **Sunday 27th September 2009**
Venue : **North Acton Playing Fields**
Competition : **WELAFA Division One**

Nice Fridge Locomotiv   2 vs 5   **Fernhead Rovers**

Jez Mahon
Tony Bunce

Three injuries, five goals and still no points - I think that basically sums up the day.

We lost our third game of the season 5-2 against Fernhead Rovers. However, for the majority of the first half and the start of the second we really did play some good football and probably should have gone in at half time two, three or four ahead.

Following a few early saves from Pete we went behind against the run of play. For the rest of the half we did everything but score. Step, Tony, Sameer and Shogo linked up brilliantly throughout and created chance after chance, but just could not put any away.

Despite conceding early on in the second half as well, we re-grouped and got ourselves back in the game with two quick goals. The first was a screamer from Jez from all of 35yrds - the goalkeeping was less than desirable but we won't take that away from Jez. The second came a few minutes later with a close finish from Tony. We pushed for the third, hit the post twice and their keeper in the face from two yards once, but just could not find it. A late third from Fernhead really hit us hard - our heads dropped and we went on to concede two more soft goals while trying to find a way back into things.

The defeat is certainly hard to take, but we can be more than happy with the first half performance. We showed exactly what we are capable of and with just a bit more composure in front of goal could have had the game wrapped up.

Having three injuries also made things difficult. Matty decided to go against evolution and see if hands work better with fingers at a different angle. The outcome.... negative, they don't! Adam then thought it would be a good idea to cut up half of his body whilst making a tackle. Once again, bad idea! Whereas Tony, on the other hand, stubbed his toe (or something like that anyway) and we all know that that really hurts, so our thoughts are with you mate!!!

Date : **Sunday 4th October 2009**
Venue : **South Park**
Competition : **WELAFA Division One**

Nice Fridge Locomotiv   1 vs 2   Facile Tigre
Pete Sharp

Finally we have some good news... we are no longer bottom of the league! Those of you that played on Sunday may be slightly confused by this, but we should be very grateful of the Chefchaouen Berbers - they quite brilliantly tonked Fat Cats 7-0, meaning that they are now bottom with no points and a minus twelve goal difference. Us, on the other hand, only minus nine - GET IN THERE!!!

Now, the game.... we took a deserved lead in the first half. I think Pete is going to claim the goal (he insists that it was on target before the keeper threw it into his own net!), but credit should go to Shogo for a perfectly timed through ball. Once again, we should have gone in at half time two or three up, but let Facile Tigre back into with a sloppy goal from a set-piece. Although I can't remember exactly, it was probably from a long throw being that that was all they had going forward!!!

The second half was quite a cagey affair with both sides having chances. You can't help but feel that if confidence was slightly higher, we would be scorer goals for fun at the moment - we are certainly creating plenty of chances, just can't put them away.

But, as has been our luck this season so far we conceded to literally the last kick of the game - and what a goal it was!! One of those things, absolutely nothing you can do about it...

I would like to give special credit to (1) Adam for a faultless and solid performance at centre back and (2) Michael for a very creative second half performance with some great through-balls that will eventually get us plenty of goals. However Man of the Match without a doubt this week was Paul. He won absolutely everything in the air and 99% of his tackles on the ground - other than the one where he did his best to break their winger in half and somehow got a goal kick for it. A fine effort!

Date : **Sunday 11th October 2009**
Venue : **Dulwich College**
Competition : **Challenge Trophy Second Round**

Nice Fridge Locomotiv 3 vs 3 AFC Millbank
AFC Millbank win 4-2 on penalties
Sameer Joomun
Ross Jenner
Michael Rowden

Where can I start? What a game... what a performance... what effort... what heartbreak...

For most it was a dreaded journey 'South of the River.' Mix in the fact it was a 10am KO (trust me Jez, it really was a 10am start!!!) and that there was a half marathon in Regents Park, the start of the day was certainly eventful. And there was a Fridge first - a real/proper/genuine (delete as applicable) warm-up involving one touch passing and closing down. Amazing!

As we have done in most games this season, we started brightly and soon took an early lead - a cool finish from Sameer after rounding the keeper. However, Millbank slowly worked their way back into the game and equalised midway through the first half. The rest of the half was end to end, but Millbank took the lead just before the break - a decent finish lobbing a semi-stranded Pete.

From a neutral point of view, the second half was pure entertainment. From my point of view, watching you lot put every bit of energy into getting an equaliser, it was anything but entertainment. The half was pretty open with both teams having plenty of chances, but it was clear that we were not going to collapse like in previous weeks. Chance after chance came and went and then... they got a penalty. Big Trev (aka Joleon Lescott) stepped up and somehow managed to get it closer to the corner flag than the post. Everyone was clearly lifted and we were still in the game. As the minutes ticked away, Ross somehow found himself in the Millbank penalty area and through shear grit and determination bundled the ball into the back of the net. This won't mean anything to most of you, but Ross therefore takes a one goal lead in the infamous *Jenner-Ellis Shield.* All to do now Chris!!

We held out until full time and started extra time with momentum in our favour. However, against the run of play Millbank once again took the lead right at the end of the first half. We re-grouped and knew that we had fifteen minutes (well, ten minutes but that's because the ref didn't want to play the full time allocation) to get ourselves back into this. As the second half of extra time went on, it seemed that the goal was just not going to come. That is until Michael picked up the ball 25yards out. There was about thirty seconds left in the game. He cut inside and curled an absolute peach of a finish into the far top corner. The keeper was left helpless. There was pandemonium in the stands. A stunning strike! It had finished 3-3 AET. We were going to penalties.

Unfortunately it was not meant to be. Both Pete and Tony missed their spotkicks and, despite a decent penalty save from Pete, it was too little too late. Final Score: AFC Millbank wiin 4-2 on penalties.

At times, the performance was stunning. For the full 120mins it was gritty, determined and committed. Everybody deserves a mention but I will give special credit to Sameer and Jez who played through a good 50% of the game with niggling injuries. However, Man of the Match this week goes to Ross who ran tirelessly for the whole game, not only getting a very well deserved goal but also tracking back and making more than a few last ditch challenges.

Date : **Sunday 8th November 2009**
Venue : **Tooting Bec**
Competition : **WELAFA Division One**

Nice Fridge Locomotiv   4   vs   1   **Facile Tigre**

Pete Sharp
Tony Bunce
Ross Jenner
Pete Sharp

On Sunday we BEAT Facile Tigre 4-1 in what can only be described as a solid and committed performance all round.

Everyone was surprisingly very upbeat and confident at kick-off and it proved accurate as Pete put us into the lead within the first minute with a fine low finish across the keeper. Shortly after, the lead was doubled by Tony, following some great link up play down the right between Pete and Huw.

There was only one team in it and it could have been three, four or even five within the first twenty minutes. However, the ref then decided to give what can only be described as a generous penalty, following an apparent handball by Matty. Fear not though young Fridgers, I was back in goal and in true Bradley Ambridge penalty-style..... it was saved!!! (yes Omer, saved!) However, Facile Tigre did soon pull one back - an unlucky deflection that was definitely not deserved.

We re-grouped and within minutes had restored the two goal lead. Pete sneaked a free-kick around the outside of the wall only to find it come straight back off the post. Luckily, Ross was in the right place to tap it away and take a two goal lead in the Chris Ellis-Ross Jenner Trophy! Even more to do now Chris...

At half time there was nothing to change. It was a case of doing the same again and not getting complacent. The second half was more of a contest, although our goal wasn't really threatened. Mid-way through the half Pete got his second, and our fourth, of the game - a great finish from the edge of the box.

The game was won and it was a case of just seeing out the half without conceding. No problem for the new, improved Fridge!!!

A great performance all round. When there was time to play some football, we did. When it needed someone to put their foot through it... Adam and Paul were usually there! I'm going to give Man of the Match this week to Abs for not only a very solid display, but also for his constant talking, motivating and encouragement for the whole 90mins. This is something that we have missed this season so far!

Date : **Sunday 15th November 2009**
Venue : **Wormwood Scrubs**
Competition : **WELAFA Division One**

Nice Fridge Locomotiv   4 vs 4   **Hampstead SDA**
Pete Sharp
Pete Sharp
Pete Sharp
Tony Bunce

Sunday saw a cracking game finish Nice Fridge 4 vs 4 Hampstead SDA.

Yes, we did take a three goal lead. Yes, we should have won. Yes, it was disappointing to concede in the last minute, but let's look at the positives. We would have been delighted with a point a few weeks ago, so to come away feeling dejected shows how far we have come along. It's a game unbeaten and it gives us something to build on - let's put a decent run together now!

To be fair, we were outplayed for the majority of the first half (to a decent footballing side I might add) but somehow went in two goals up - both good, composed finishes from Pete. This was quickly turned into three at the start of the 2nd half as Pete superbly completed his hat-trick. The Nice Fridge from the start of the season then reappeared for a while. We got scrappy, started losing the challenges again and before we knew it, it was 3-3.

Tony gave us a relatively late lead with a stunning finish from all of 35yrds - a looping effort, leaving the keeper stranded (whilst, still being on his line... is that even possible?!?)

Hampstead SDA continued to press and, although it is difficult to admit, got what was probably a deserved equaliser right at the death. I must say that it was good to see everyone trying to cheer eachother up at the end and not blaming one another - it's this sort of team spirit that will give us that extra 10%.

A special mention this week should go to Matty for a superb battling performance in the middle of the park, made even harder by the state of the pitch. However, I think it is only fair to the Man of the Match award to Pete. A great hat-trick and great link-up play with Tony throughout giving us plenty of attacking threat.

Date : **Sunday 13th December 2009**
Venue : **South Park**
Competition : **WELAFA Division One**

Nice Fridge Locomotiv   3 vs 2   Old Theonians
Step Sharp
Pete Sharp
Sameer Joomun

Sunday was our last game before Christmas. I think it is fair to say that despite it being the time of goodwill and all that, there was very little of it on the pitch. It was an entertaining, well-fought battle and I am delighted to say that we deservedly came out on top. Before getting onto the game itself, I think we should give a special mention to the sniper that was hiding in one of the trees for the whole game. Personally, I reckon he did a great job of putting their two strikers on the deck for 90mins! Great accuracy.

The game started at a fast pace but we were quickly into our stride, playing the sort of football that has not been seen at The Withdean since Charlton came and conquered. The link-up between Abs, Huw and Step was first class and we spent the first 20mins camped in their half. We soon took the lead with Step's first goal of the season, rounding off a solid move by following in his own shot that was superbly saved by their keeper.

The game then opened up a bit more and the game was soon leveled up - a 'convincing' 25yard that left Neil stranded and with no chance (us goalkeepers need to stick together, alright?!?). Two moments of contraversy followed : firstly their jelly-legged striker chased down a poor goalkick from Neil before scuffing his shot and then collapsing in a heap on the floor. He appealed for the penalty, we called him a cheat. All seemed fair until at half-time Neil claimed "he did dive, but I caught him with my trailing hand." How does that work then Neil?!? At the other end, we had our own penalty shout, but this one was blatant. The defender spun round and parried it to the ground not once, but twice. No penalty given.

Then came the goal of the season so far (sorry Tony, it was definitely better than your 35 yarder against the blind keeper). Neil drop kicked the ball towards their back line, where Jez won the first flick on to Tony. The ball was then played back to Jez who calmly lifted it over the defender into Pete's path, who cooly placed it over the advancing keeper's head and into the back of the net.

HALF TIME 2-1

We made two changes at half time - Sameer on for Tony to give us some extra pace upfront and Chris on for the injured Abs. They made a few changes as well and started the half pretty strongly, without really threatening our goal. Not a lot happened until they got a penalty midway through the half - Chris supposedly pushing someone twice his size (that's height, rather than width) in the back. They scored and it was game-on!

We stepped up a few gears again and were soon creating more and more chances, the most noticeably being Sameer who could not get the ball out of his feet quick enough to find a finish. However, as all good strikers do, if you miss an easy chance why not go and score the difficult one. The long throws from Chris were causing all sorts of problems and one finally paid off as Sameer got to one first to brilliantly place his header into the bottom corner. Chris then got a bit too confident and even hit the crossbar direct from a throw.

We defended resolutely for the last ten minutes or so and held on for a thoroughly well-deserved three points.

FULL TIME 3-2

We are now unbeaten in four and up to fifth in the table. There is a fair gap between us and Facile Tigre in fourth, but they are more that catcheable.

Date : **Sunday 14th February 2010**
Venue : **South Park**
Competition : **WELAFA Division One**
Report written by Pete Sharp

Nice Fridge Locomotiv   6 vs 2   Hampstead SDA
Omer Kutluoglu
Omer Kutluoglu
Paul Pearman
Paul Pearman
Paul Pearman
Martin Hill

It is with enormous pleasure I can announce that on the morning of Valentines Day 2010, Nice Fridge Lokomotiv continued their love affair with the WELAFA Div 1 Challenge Cup!

Allow me to set the scene… it was a chilly, overcast morning, no sunshine, no rain, no wind. The pitch was soft, but flat. The ref, on time (but with no understanding of the offside rule). The oppo, depleted (I'll get to that in a minute), late, but ready for battle. At 9:45, 13 Fridgers marched out from their warm changing room focussed and ready for battle. The warm up was gentle, yet thorough. As we fired in some crosses and shots towards our stand-in goalie, we thought to ourselves "is this the first decent keeper to ever pull on a QPR goalie jersey"? I'd set the team out to defend and counter attack, with our main tactic to send the big lads forward to attack Martin's long throw. Then our former great leader, strolled out onto the turf at 10:05 and announced the oppo only had 9. The ref then let out a blast of his (very annoying) whistle to summon the captains. As one, our team turned to see that there were only 3 of the oppo warming up! We turned the other way to see the other 6 (one of which looked as so he needed a stretcher, or at least some crutches) stroll out casually onto the South Park turf.

The game kicked off, with the Fridge firmly in control. Marshalled by our midfield maestro and captain Matty, we pulled the oppo from one side of the pitch to the other with accurate and sensible passing creating several decent chances, most of which were spurned by myself. It was suggested by someone on our team that we should give them one of our lads "to make a game of it". After glancing over at our bench (which by the way could have easily been the shortest group of subs ever to play football), I dismissed that notion immediately, and instructed the gentleman in question to "not be such a plank". Then, out of nowhere, the oppo counter attacked, and had a half chance which their lad fired over the bar. At that point, the gentleman from earlier suggested we were being too negative, and needed to get a few extra bodies forward. I was dubious, but decided to heed the advice of the experienced one, and move Step from CB into midfield, and move Martin up top taking us from a 4-4-2 to a 3-4-3. While we were in that transitional period, we went one down, so I immediately switched back to the original formation, and therefore exonerate myself of any responsibility! They bought on a 10th man, but the rest of the half played out like the game had started, with us in control. And we scored twice, both goals scored by Omer. The old master showing he still has an eye for goal with a neat finish from a decent through ball (apologies, can't remember who) and a header from all of 6 inches out which was made all the more impressive as he shoved several of our lads out of the way to poach his second goal. Their keeper repelled us for the rest of the half making several decent saves, the two most notable being a save at full stretch from an Omer "bicycle kick" (yes, you've read that right) to deny the big man his hat-trick, and going in for a 50-50 with me using his head!

Half time, and I took Abs off for Shogo, and hauled myself off and brought on Paul (Tony's cousin) to play up top alongside Omer. This seemed to work a treat, as Paul got on the end of an Omer cross, and with a diving header sent the ball past the despairing dive of their keeper and into the bottom corner. Now, I'm not sure how tall Paul is, but I think he is probably the shortest player to score a header for the Fridge, a record I believe was held previously by Shogo. At 3-1, we were cruising until, disaster struck! The ref awarded them a penalty, citing a (blatant) push on their striker by Adam. Despite Adam protesting his innocence, the referees mind was made up and their lad confidently placed the ball on the spot. In an effort to delay proceedings a bit longer, I made a cheeky sub, bringing on Jermaine for Omer. But I don't think anyone noticed and it certainly didn't faze their penalty taker. With the ball on the spot, the lad shaped to strike it left footed. The ref blasted on his whistle, a silence broke out across London , as a City nervously waited the outcome of this pivotal moment. He arced his run round to the left and hit a ferocious right-footed shot, kept out magnificently by Tony! As we leapt in celebration, we looked up to see the ball looping back towards their penalty taker. Tony leapt to his feet and charged out towards the ball, and in slow-motion, their lad scuffed the ball agonisingly wide! 3-1, and we were favourites again. We scored two more, both from little Paul, completing his hat-trick with two very decent right-footed finishes, showing everybody that had missed previously (me, mainly) how to stick the ball in the net. Our 6th was scored by Martin, a low right-footed finish in the near post after sending the keeper the wrong way. The game finished 6-2, I can't remember at which point their last goal went in, but no-one really wants to read about that do they?

Now onto the MOM award. Paul (the short one), not only for his debut hat-trick, but for giving the oppo endless headaches with his tireless work rate and bags of pace. A deserved MOM IMO. Omer, with his goals and an assist seems to save his best form for the cup. Adam had a decent game down the right and Step and Paul (the taller one) worked very well together in the centre of our defence. Tony didn't have a lot to do, but when called upon made a few decent saves in the second half on top of his penalty heroics. Jermaine didn't see much of the ball on his debut, but looked to have plenty of pace and worked hard off the ball working well with Shogo to repel their attacks down our left side.

Date : **Sunday 21st February 2010**
Venue : **Wormwood Scrubs**
Competition : **WELAFA Division One**

Nice Fridge Locomotiv   2 vs 0   Old Theonians
Pete Sharp
Omer Kutluoglu

Imagine the scene if you will - Wormwood Scrubs, bright blue skies, pleasant sunshine, cool breeze, Highbury-esque green carpet of a playing surface, hot water in the showers ...... well it was nothing like that!!

The morning started with a random text message advising that there was half a foot of snow at Omer Mansions. All we had in Dartford was torrential rain. On arrival the talk was all about whether the game would actually go ahead - other teams were bringing the nets back to the changing rooms and trudging back to their cars, but not us. We were determined to find a pitch that would be deemed 'playable.' It came down to a choice between a perfect looking kids pitch or a fullsize one that ONLY had half a dozen puddles - as I wasn't playing and didn't really care, the 'puddle pitch' won. Trust me, if I had been in goal we would have been playing on the kid's pitch!!

The game kicked off (half an hour late - we'll say that it was to give the pitch time to dry out, but the truth is the ref was ridiculously late!) and it was a pretty scrappy affair at first. Both teams were prepared to get stuck in and the defences were on top for the first 20mins or so. We started to create a few openings, with little Paul and Huw working well down the wings and Martin and Neil getting stuck in in the middle. In truth, other than a decent save from Tony towards the end of the half it was fairly even-stevens!

At half time Huw was subbed off for Jez and the team instructions were simply 'keep it coming!'

Despite the pitch starting to seriously cut up, the energy levels were still just as high and we soon got our reward. Pete had earlier missed a one-on-one that he would have backed himself to score, but made up for it with a well controlled header at the backpost that the keeper had misjudged. Usually at this stage we manage to sit back, make some mistakes and let the oppo get back into the game, but we kept the tempo up and committed ourselves to every challenge. The pitch was probably bordering on unplayable at this stage but we made the most of the wings - first with little Paul causing all sorts of trouble and then Shogo following in the same footsteps when they subbed for eachother half way through the half.

The defence were solid throughout and even if any half-chances did get through, Tony was on hand to tidy anything up. The second and deciding goal came in the very last minute. We broke in numbers and Omer found himself five yards out with the ball at his feet, two defenders around him and the keeper on his line. As much as it pains me to say this, rather than rushing his chance Omer cooly turned the ball away from the defender and struck it high into the roof of the net.

It had been a hard-fought game but we deservedly won 2-0. There were a number of players that could have been given Man of the Match this week, but for his sheer determination and battling in the middle (and the fact that he has only been back from injury for two weeks) it goes to MARTIN, but the defence (and Tony) should take credit for our first clean sheet of the season.

Date : **Sunday 14th March 2010**
Venue : **Tooting Fishponds**
Competition : **WELAFA Division One**

Nice Fridge Locomotiv 4 vs 1 Fat Cats
Step Sharp
Pete Sharp
Jez Mahon
Pete Sharp

The game today was nothing short of epic. Given the circumstances, given the situation and given the events it was undoubtedly the performance of the season so far. Before I get onto the game I would also like to give a special mention to the support that came to watch - eight fans in total I believe (quite possibly a Fridge record!).

Right, let's see how much of this I can remember. We started with a bare eleven after Martin got injured playing on Saturday and Little Paul went AWOL. Shogo arrived with about two minutes to spare and Jez's mate (Kev) with about 30secs to go - we were just about ready to kick off.

The first half was a fairly open encounter. Both teams had their chances but we were certainly on top. Then it got interesting - Nick went down injured after falling in a pothole (!!!), closely followed by Kev who pulled a muscle and then Tony in goal who had been nursing a groin injury before kickoff. However, credit where credit is due, all three battled on and Nick even had the positivity to come out with "I can run but it is just when I kick it that it hurts." As the half went on we were creating more and more chances with Shogo and Matty causing absolute chaos down our left wing and Jez pinging some cracking deliveries into the area.

Our opener came on the stroke of half time - Shogo battled hard down the left to dispossess their right back and saw his shot well saved by their keeper, only for the rebound to pop up for Step to bravely head home. If he tries to convince anybody that he leapt four foot off the ground to get to the ball, we have video footage to prove that his feet did not leave the floor. One nil up at half time and all was looking good... until....

As we gathered behind the goal Jez ran (well, limped) straight for the Deep Heat and happily emptied the entire tube onto his right thigh. Then Matty decided to break the news to everyone that his hamstring "had gone." There was no way that he could continue. So we were going to be playing the second half (up hill I might add) with ten men. Ten men that included an injured Tony, Kev, Nick and Jez (oh and Abs had apparently hurt his finger!!). It was going to be tough!!

We had agreed to sit slightly deeper and soak up the pressure for a bit. So Pete went straight up the other end and beat their keeper to put us two nil up (with a bit of help from their defender, but Pete says that it was on target anyway so who are we to judge). Once again, we agreed to take it easy and conserve energy. This time Jez took the ball and shot from twenty yards - it was certainly powerful but was straight at the keeper. But this wasn't any keeper, this was a keeper that basically turned round and rolled the ball into his own net - perfectly complimented by Jez's celebration of shaking his head and laughing, before confirming that he WAS going to be claiming it! THREE NIL UP but still pretty much a whole half to go.

The next twenty minutes were fairly boring when compared to the rest of the game. We were solid at the back and knew that we did not have to press particularly hard going forward. Then came a potential turning point - our very own Abs 'Vinnie Jones' Calim wanted to make a name for himself and basically assaulted their centre forward. I'm sure that he did something to deserve such a reaction, but he was as shocked as the rest of us. Despite some pointless appealing, the ref showed a straight red card and we were now down to NINE MEN for the last part of the game.

With about three minutes to go they got a consolation from a decent move that caught us somewhat tired. However, straight from kick-off Kev back-heeled it to Pete who hit a forty yard pass out to Shogo on the left. He cut inside the defender and unluckily saw his effort come off of the inside of the post - so unlucky and would certainly have been a Goal of the Season contender. A few moments later and Pete was in exactly the same position down the left. He also cut inside but this time calmly placed the ball in the far corner. There was barely time to restart before hearing the full time whistle. Nice Fridge win 4-1.

Everyone should be immensely proud of themselves. Many thanks to those who battled on through the pain barrier and many thanks to the rest who each put in that extra 20% to make up for their injured teammates. I don't think anyone will disagree with this, but Man of the Match this week goes to SHOGO. A stunning performance from minute one, that had their defence running all over the place.

Date : **Sunday 11th April 2010**
Venue : **South Park**
Competition : **The Nice Fridge Shield**
Written by Pete Sharp

Nice Fridge Locomotiv   2   vs   2   Nice Fridge Veterans
Locomotiv win 4-3 on penalties
Pete Sharp
Pete Sharp

Sunday saw the inaugural Fridge vs Fridge encounter which fittingly took place at the spiritual home of The Fridge, nay, the home of football... South Park. The conditions were perfect; the pitch was flat and dry, and bathed in bright London sunshine. We arrived at the changing rooms only to be greeted by some of the greats of The Fridge past and present. Gruber, Colin, Andy, Seb, Martinez, Nawaz, Mitch, the list goes on. Oh, Omer and Jez turned out as well! Old Fridge also bought a huge support, easily the highest attendance of the season. As Brad was giving his team talk, we were all distracted by the antics coming from the other end. They had a team photo, Champions League stylee! I have honestly not seen anything like it!

Anyway, onto the game... The Old Fridge started well, with Jez (of all people) pulling the strings in the centre of their midfield. We were struggling to keep hold of the ball for any period of time, as the oppo matched our work rate all over the pitch making life difficult for us. We did defend well however as Brad didn't have too much to deal with. They went a goal up after Omer found himself one on one with Brad, and then squared it for their other forward to slide in (apologies, can't remember who scored). I know what you're all thinking… "Omer, passing the ball?" Believe me I'm as confused as anyone; I have never experienced such an anomaly. We equalised a few minutes later after a long throw-in from Martin on the left looped into the area, and their defence (Seb, Colin and Andy) inexplicably and uncharacteristically let it bounce! I couldn't believe my luck as I nicked in unmarked from the back post to head into the net from 6 yards. The other highlights of the half were Jez and Nawaz missing with shots that threatened the corner flags more than Brad's goal!

Second half began in much the same vein with Old Fridge more than matching their younger, fitter, more talented (!!!) counterparts! They created several decent chances, but Brad and his back four were more than equal to all they threw at us. Its good to have Brad back by the way isn't it? Anyway, Old Fridge took the lead again through Omer (I think) with a neat turn and finish from close range. That goal I believe takes the old master to 100 Fridge goals, which is truly remarkable for a man of his shape and such little talent (only joking Omer, great work)! We responded by moving Paul from centre half to midfield, which turned out to be inspired as he immediately had an impact. It was his pinpoint cross that picked me out (completely unmarked again, what was Colin doing?) to head the equaliser towards the end. It was Old Fridge who finished stronger, with Jez and Nawaz in particular causing the problems with decent passing and direct runs. The last 30 seconds we were defending for our lives, as Neil put in a terrific last ditch challenge to deny a certain goal inside our 6 yard box, and after a couple of half clearances and blocked shots, Brad terrifically got down to his right and tipped a decent effort round the post.

A draw was perhaps a bit of a flattering result for us, but it was an enjoyable game played in good spirit. We decided to settle the game on penalties, which we won 4-3 with Brad and Andy making decent saves, although I have to say Brad looked a good 3 or 4 inches off his line when making that save… the dirty cheat!

Date : **Sunday 18th April 2010**
Venue : **Warren Farm**
Competition : **WELAFA Division One**

Nice Fridge Locomotiv   1   vs   5   **Chefchaoun Berbers**
Martin Hill

Today we played against The Berbers. Although they have not won the league this year, I think we would all agree that they are without doubt the best footballing side in the division. The result finished 5-1 but that is nowhere near the full story.

On the hottest day of the year so far, eleven Nice Fridge warriors arrived at the ground to find the oppo doing an incredibly thorough warm-up. Ours consisted of running across the pitch and then a few stretches - only for Omer to comment (whilst we were walking to the halfway line to start) that he was already tired. Trust me, there is more of that shortly!!

After seeing them kick off and completely about thirty passes, we finally touched the ball! We were battling hard but to no avail. We soon went one and then two nil down. In truth, the goals were probably avoidable but it is easier said than done at this level. Then Omer decided that he had enough and didn't want to play anymore - he claimed that his groin had "gone" but make of that what you will. So... two nil down after 25mins, playing the best team in then league and now ten men. Oh the fun!

We continued to battle and work for one another but did concede one more before half time, this time a screamer that you can't really do a lot about. The highlight of our half was a stunning 25 yard effort from Pete that rattled the crossbar with the keeper looking more stranded than a British tourist trying to get home (topical joke there, you see). Oh by the way, as the half came to an end Martin also went off for a few minutes with an injury and Abs was struggling as well!

At half time it was agreed that the win was probably now out of the question. We were to go out and fight for one another and make sure that it did not become a cricket score. And it didn't, although we certainly tried our best to get them towards double-figures.

Despite starting the half the stronger of the two, it was the Berbers who got the next goal. A corner came in and Huw swung a foot at it to get it clear. Except, the ball span erratically towards myself but there was nothing to worry about as I was well-positioned (obviously!) Well that would have been the case if I had chosen to catch the ball and not let it spill into the bottom corner. After some friendly discussion at full time, it was agreed that it would go down as my own goal and not Huw's so sorry about that lads!

We had played approx 250mins of football against these guys at this stage and the aggregate score was 14-0, but that was about to change. We were awarded an indirect free-kick (following an alleged backpass) about seven yards out and Martin stepped up with confidence. They positioned there entire team on the goal line but that didn't phase Martin - if in doubt, just fire it hard into the top left hand corner. Easy. 4-1. We were back in it!

Well not really, they went up the other end and scored a fifth with a bit of help from Adam who weighed up his options of clearing the ball off of the line and decided to just completely miss it and end up on his backside. What a sight!

Both teams had further chances but the heat was starting to slow everyone down and the ref soon blew his whistle to the relief of ten shattered Fridgeonians. The result obviously doesn't suggest it, but it was a super performance throughout. Man of the Match though this week goes to Pete - I'm not sure he stopped running for the entire 90mins and probably covered 99% of the pitch at some point.

Date : **Sunday 9th May 2010**
Venue : **Hanwell Town Football Club**
Competition : **The Sportsmanship Shield Cup Final**

Nice Fridge Locomotiv   2   vs   0   AFC Millbank
Adam Bunce
Martin Hill

Where shall I start? I suppose inside our own penalty area would be a good place being that we spent at least 75mins of the game camped there, defending for our lives.

From the first whistle we were under pressure - Millbank came forward in numbers. They tried to force their ways through the middle; they failed. They tried to work in down the wings; they failed. They tried to score from a ridiculous number of corners; they failed.

Our midfield worked tirelessly throughout and broke down a lot of their rhythm. When they did get through the midfield the back four were on hand to clear away any danger. Despite all of their pressure, I can honestly say that they only really got into our area on a few occasions - after all, for all their possession in the first half, I only had two saves to make!

We knew our chance would come. And come it did! A wicked free-kick out on the right wing from Tony was simply undefendable and gave Adam the simple task of smashing/scuffing the ball home. One chance, one goal - that's how you play football!

The biggest shock came at half time - not only did we get to go back into a changing room but we were also supplied with a jug of orange squash. Hanwell Town Football Club - what a place!!!

We knew that the second half would be the same, if not harder, than the first. We had proven that we could do it for 45mins and certainly had every intention of doing it again. Millbank came forward attack after attack, player after player but were greeted by a Nice Fridge Brick Wall! To be honest, there really isn't that much to say. If you want minute by minute updates, please feel free to read the previous sentence twenty times. Then, heartbreak... for them (I had you there didn't I??). With literally the last kick of the game we completed the perfect counter attack. Tony played an inch perfect pass to Pete (before acting dead for some reason) who played the ball into the feet of Martin to cooly slot home the winner. The scenes were incredible - this is no exaggeration, there were literally three fans celebrating! Incredible!

As it is a special event, I'm going to attempt to give every player a match analysis:

Abs Calim - Spent the whole game keeping the back four together perfectly. Took complete control of organising corners and took out/tackled Juda as and when required.
Nick Sharp - Could potentially have been made to look very silly by Juda, but simply stood his ground and made him resort to diving to try and win penalties. Simple but easily the most effective way!
Paul Burnham - This could be for any game this season. Won absolutely everything in the air and on the floor. Finished an unfortunate second in the Tackle of The Match Award...
Adam Bunce - Scored his first every Nice Fridge goal and, as above, won absolutely everything in the air and on the ground. Winner of the Tackle of The Match Award and collected a yellow card in the process. Please remember that this was the Sportsmanship Shield (!!!)
Martin Hill - A quiet first half due to our constant defending but worked tirelessly to open up the play and came into his own in the second half with some superb counter attacking and tackling. And let's not forget about the enormous throws.
Jez Mahon - Was given Man of the Match by (in his own words) "an old and slightly senile ref." A superb mixture of flair and simplicity when required.
Neil Colquhoun - On a personal level I want to say a big thanks for two great team talks before the game and at half time. Controlled the middle effortlessly and kept everyone together. Sat in front of the defence to stop anything getting through - and I mean anything!
Matty Russell - This one game is a summary of his whole season! The Captain leads by example - winning every challenge, covering every blade of grass and supporting the team throughout. Unfortunately went off injured again but was still a key influence from the touchline

Tony Bunce - Played out of position on the right wing. Did not complain once and looked as if he had been there his whole career. A superb free-kick for the first goal and perfect through-ball for the second. Linked up brilliantly with Abs down the right and was involved in every chance we had - as I say, the two goals!!!
Pete Sharp - Probably had the hardest task of the day. Played upfront on his own and ran his socks off. He held the ball up at every opportunity and consistently won free-kicks and throws to give the team time to join him. Even found the energy to drop back and defend for the last ten minutes.
Huw Allanson - Came on as sub for Matty and got stuck in straight away. Was just the defensive minded option that we needed to hold on at the end. Was also a key influence on the touchline in the first half.

This is probably the hardest decision of the season and, in truth, everybody deserves man of the match but this week it goes to Nick. It's very difficult to explain his performance as he made it look so simple but I think all of the other players will agree that he made Juda look very ordinary at times!

And The Winner Is...

Every respectable organisation, no matter what level they are operating at, needs to have an Annual General Meeting. It gives all of the members an opportunity to express their feelings, suggest ways in which things can be improved, discuss which direction the company is going in and often involves the appointing and re-appointing of roles such as chairman, treasurer and secretary. And if you believe that is what happened at our AGM then you are sorely mistaken. For a Sunday league football team it is nothing more than an excuse to get together and have a drink, or ten.

Strangely enough this would be only the second AGM that the club had arranged in all of the years that I had been involved. During that event I was presented with the David Seaman award for being lobbed during at least five games that season – the trophy itself was great but I suppose the reasoning behind it isn't really something to be proud of.

I wanted to make the night as enjoyable as possible and, being the sad perfectionist that I am, even wrote down the order that the trophies would be presented in. Yes, there would be a lot of trophies – I wanted to make sure that all of the regulars were awarded with something. It would also be an ideal opportunity to win over any players that still had doubts in my managerial ability, although I was fairly confident that none of these still existed – we had just won the cup, remember.

The AGM had been planned for at least three months now and I had spent most evenings either choosing the trophies, deciding on the categories and winners and then organising the quiz for the night. The big concern with arranging something like this is that everybody tends to say yes when the idea is first put forward, but then as soon as you give definitive details the excuses start to come out as to why they will not be there. Luckily for me I clearly have a decent group of players, with Ross, Martin and Neil the only three that could not make it. In Neil's defence, he was genuinely disappointed to be missing the night and even tried to rearrange various flights back from Italy to get there on time.

Pete agreed to take control of the evening and, in turn, became the quiz-master. The group was split into four teams consisting of Tony, Abs, Paul and Adam in one, Matty, Shogo, Chris and Dan Mantini in another, Huw, Jez and Omer in the third, with Step and Nick making up the fourth.

With the results counted and verified, the teams of Abs and Step were tied for the lead despite only getting a disappointing fourteen out of thirty-seven correct. Either I had made the questions a bit too difficult or the team were living up to the rumours of footballers having a low IQ. Why don't you try the quiz for yourself on the next few pages?

There was only one logical way for the winner to be ultimately decided. Step and Abs would go head-to-head with the first to down a pint taking the title. Well, this was possibly the most one-sided contest in history with Abs having his drink finished by the time Step had even got it to his mouth.

After each round of the quiz Pete and myself presented a trophy to one 'lucky' recipient. The majority of the awards were just 'fun' ones, either remembering a funny event from the season or brining up something that the winner would rather we all forget. We then obviously had the serious and prestigious trophies such as Goal of The Season, Golden Boot and Player of The Year. Unfortunately the Sky cameras were not available to broadcast the evening, so the winners and 'losers' were as follows:

Abs Calim – Vinnie Jones Award (for *that* challenge in the game against Fat Cats)
Martin Hill – Rory Delap Award (self explanatory really isn't it)
Chris Ellis – Own Goal of The Season (a fine finished against Barnet Eagles earlier on in the season)
Huw Allanson – Worst Performance of The Season (responsible for seven of the eight we conceded against Barnet Eagles)
Step Sharp – John O'Shea Award (he played in every position)
Shogo Hirata - Toy Car Award (was presented with a toy car as had suffered from car trouble throughout the season)
Adam Bunce – 'If In Doubt' Award (every clearance goes at least fifty yards out of play)

Jez Mahon – Nick Barmby Award (his best years are officially behind him)
Matty Russell – Darren Anderton Award (for his incredible finger injury earlier on in the season)
Neil Colquhoun – Ultimate Professional Award (for all of his help with team talks and tactics)
Ross Jenner – Jenner/Ellis Shield (Chris and Ross had started a competition for who could score more. Ross won 2-0)
Omer Kutluoglu – A Century of Goals (a very proud award to present to a Nice Fridge legend)
Pete Sharp – Golden Boot (scoring an impressive fifteen goals)
Nick Sharp – Most Improved Player (as voted for by the team)
Tony Bunce – Goal of The Season (a forty yard half volley)
Paul Burnham – Player of The Season (an absolute rock at centre back)

At the end of the evening there was no doubt that it had been a success. Everybody had enjoyed themselves and I could finally relax knowing that all of the stress and effort had been worth it. I could almost see my name being written up on the Nice Fridge Legends Board – forget the Centurions Board at Lords Cricket Ground, this is the one to get on!

So, the season was officially over. We never did actually pick up the Sportsmanship Shield in the end. At the time of the AGM I was holiday and Huw, who was intending to go in my absence, got stuck up in Birmingham with work. To be honest, it is probably for the best as the trophy is so large that it would take up half of the space in my flat. We didn't need it though – we all had our medals from the day and, more importantly, had the memories and knowledge that we were the Sportsmanship Shield Cup Winners. Potentially, we could be the holders of this award for a very long time as it is only likely to be dusted off again if the weather causes problems. On second thoughts, this is England, so it will probably be up for grabs again in May 2011.

As promised, you can now have a go at the quiz yourself. It was broken down into six rounds and the answers can be found at the end of this book. However, please bare in mind that this quiz took place in May 2010 and that some of the answers may no longer be correct. In fact, give yourselves an extra point if you can work out the answers to any questions that have since changed. Please be aware that the answers to the first three categories can be found on page 103.

A. Grounds and Stadiums
1. What team's ground is closest to the River Mersey?
2. What is the capacity of the 'new' Wembley?
3. What is the name of West Ham United's ground?
4. What is unique about Chester City's Deva Stadium?
5. What is the only football ground to have held a cricket Test match?
6. What city is the Maracana Stadium in?

B. England
1. Who was the first England international to be sent off?
2. Who is the only England player to be sent off twice?
3. How many red roses are on the Three Lions badge?
4. What player was in the England squad for the 1996, 1998, 2000 and 2002 tournaments?
5. Who scored the only goal when Germany beat England in the last game at Old Wembley?
6. What country have England played the most international matches against?

C. Football Firsts
1. Who was the first ever substitute to be used in an English League game?
2. Who are the only non-league club to win the FA Cup?
3. Who was Britain's first £2m player?
4. What was used in the 1973 FA Cup Final, but never used again?
5. What was unique about the Chelsea vs Southampton game on 26th December 1999?
6. Which player scored the first ever Premier League goal to be screened on live TV?

D. Premier League
1. Who scored the first ever goal in the Premier League?
2. How many different clubs have played in the Premier League?
3. When Spurs beat Wigan 9-1 in November 2009, what was the score at half-time?
4. How is the song "Offside" by Barry Stroller better known?
5. Who was the first goalkeeper to score in the Premier League?
6. Name the two Premier League clubs that Wayne Rooney has not scored against (two points)

E. Tricky Trivia
1. Who has held the FA Cup for the longest period?
2. Which player scored a hat-trick for his country, but never scored for his club?
3. When did Bobby Moore score his last goal?
4. Who was the last England manager to lead a side out at the 'old' Wembley?
5. Who are the only English league club whose name contains no letters that can be coloured in?
6. Why do Germany wear green as their second choice colours?

F. Nice Fridge 2009/10 Trivia
1. How many different goalkeepers did we use during the season?
2. Who scored our first goal of 2010?
3. Who did we get our first league win against?
4. What was the score at full-time in the cup game against Millbank when we lost on penalties?
5. We scored two hat-tricks in the season. What team were they both against?
6. What is the total aggregate score of our three cup games this season?

The answers to the final three categories are on page 104.

Quiz Answers

As promised, here are the answers for the quiz that starts on page 101. Remember that the winning score at our AGM was only 14.

A. Grounds and Stadiums
1. Stockport County
2. 90,000
3. The Boleyn Ground (Not Upton Park)
4. It is in two countries. The pitch is in Wales but the main stand is in England
5. Brammall Lane
6. Rio De Janeiro

B. England
1. Alan Mullery
2. David Beckham
3. Ten
4. Gareth Southgate
5. Dietmar Hamann
6. Scotland (110 times)

C. Football Firsts
1. Keith Peacock
2. Tottenham Hotspur in 1901
3. Mark Hughes to Barcelona in 1986
4. An orange ball
5. Chelsea fielded an all foreign starting eleven
6. Teddy Sheringham

D. Premier League
1. Brian Deane
2. 43
3. 1-0 Spurs
4. Match Of The Day theme tune
5. Peter Schmeichal
6. Stoke City and Manchester United (two points)

E. Tricky Trivia
1. Portsmouth – they won it in 1939 and held it until after the war in 1946
2. Geoff Hurst – he played one cricket county championship game for Essex as wicket keeper and was out for a duck. He obviously scored a hat-trick in the 1966 World Cup Final
3. In the film 'Escape To Victory.'
4. Mike Bassett in the film England Manager
5. Hull City
6. Ireland were the first team to offer to play them after World War Two

F. Nice Fridge 2009/10 Trivia
1. Eight – Brad, Pete, Paul, Step, Neil, Omer, Tony, Adam
2. Shogo against Hampstead SDA (we lost 3-1)
3. Facile Tigre (we won 4-1)
4. 2-2
5. Hampstead SDA (Pete and Paul Pearson)
6. 9-10 (3-3, 6-2 & 0-5)

The total possible score is thirty-seven. How did you get on?

Pretty Football Isn't Everything

Here is the final league table from my first season in charge:

2009-2010 Season

West End (London) A.F.A.

Sunday AM - Division One

		P	W	D	L	F	A	Pts
1	Masons Arms (The)	16	13	2	1	65	20	41
2	Chefchaouen Berbers	16	13	1	2	74	23	40
3	Barnet Eagles	16	11	5	0	65	25	38
4	Facile Tigre	16	8	1	7	38	48	25
5	Hampstead SDA	16	6	1	9	44	47	19
6	**Nice Fridge**	**16**	**4**	**4**	**8**	**32**	**48**	**16**
7	Fat Cats	16	3	2	11	21	67	11
8	Old Theonians	16	3	1	12	22	49	10
9	Fernhead Rovers 'A'	16	2	1	13	21	55	7

The Masons Arms	4	vs	3	Nice Fridge
Barnet Eagles	8	vs	4	Nice Fridge
Fernhead Rovers	5	vs	2	Nice Fridge
Nice Fridge	1	vs	2	Facile Tigre
Nice Fridge	0	vs	5	Chefch'n Berbers
Facile Tigre	1	vs	4	Nice Fridge
Nice Fridge	4	vs	4	Hampstead SDA
Nice Fridge	1	vs	1	Barnet Eagles
Old Theonians	2	vs	3	Nice Fridge
Hampstead SDA	3	vs	1	Nice Fridge
Nice Fridge	2	vs	0	Old Theonians
Fat Cats	1	vs	4	Nice Fridge
Nice Fridge	2	vs	7	The Masons Arms
Chefch'n Berbers	5	vs	1	Nice Fridge
Nice Fridge		Draw awarded		Fernhead Rovers
Nice Fridge		Draw awarded		Fat Cats

I made the difficult, yet sensible decision to wait a few weeks before emailing the team to get the last of the outstanding subs together. What I didn't realise at this stage was exactly how hard this task would be. I was kind enough to give them all until after July pay-day, but apparently that wasn't enough. I feel it should be made clear here that Omer failed to mention this when selling the job to me all those months ago!

   The big news of the summer was that we would be getting a new sponsor for the 2010/11 season. Officially, I suppose we were still sponsored by Alternative Networks but we hadn't worn those kits for a good few seasons now and it was certainly time to move on. As explained before, we had three kits in the meantime - the navy blue Nike strip, the green and white hooped Locomotiv one and the silver and gold (actually grey and yellow) Hyde shirts. The only problem was that the Nike kit was left at Wormwood Scrubs and then lost during all of their building works and we only had ten and eleven of the Locomotiv and Hyde shirts respectively.

   It was pretty clear that we needed our identity back and thanks to Tony this was possible. It is fair to say that he managed to negotiate the deal of the century. He had convinced his company's solicitors that we were a team on the up and that this would be the best five hundred pounds they would ever spend. The deal would see us return to our traditional red and blue colours with a fancy gold trim (fortunately not too similar to that of Crystal Palace), along with the name GJ Templeman emblazoned across the front. I'm not one to be bias, but I think you will be hard pushed to find a better solicitor in the whole of the land.

   No kit would be complete without a Nice Fridge logo positioned perfectly on the heart of the shirt. This was designed by Tony and myself and it not only incorporates the club name, but also associates us to the WELAFA league with their logo at the foot of the badge. Any self-respecting team needs a catchy slogan to complete their branding image and we certainly fall into that category. Forget about "You'll Never Walk Alone" or "Be Prepared" we had taken it to the next level. At the very top of the badge, in Latin, reads the words "pulchellus lusum est non panton." For those without a Grammar School education that translates perfectly to "pretty football isn't everything." Whether you think it is genius or cheesy, you most definitely cannot argue about the accuracy. The final touch was to add an England-style star above the badge to commemorate our cup success the previous May. With all of this going on, I had completely moved away from the Nice Fridge Legends Board idea – anything less than Hollywood or Vegas would be a disappointment right now!

It was time to send another email. July was coming to an end and the new season was fast approaching – even if last season's subs were not on their way at quite the same speed. I was again feeling generous and this time gave them until August to cough up their subs for the forthcoming campaign. In my head I knew that there was no chance of this happening, so figured as long as I had everything in place by September it would give me just enough time to pay for the pitches, insurance, registration etc. This was turning into a full time job.

Surprisingly, I didn't get too many excuses as to why I wouldn't be getting their money – I was generally just ignored. One conversation I did have though still confuses me to this very day. For his own safety and humility the player can remain anonymous, but it went as follows:

"I didn't realise that I owed any money mate."

"Of course you do. You played a few games last season, didn't pay any sub at the start of the year and haven't paid any since."

"Yeah I know, but why do I owe the club money?"

Can somebody please explain to me what the best response to this would be? I shall give him the benefit of the doubt that he has mis-interpreted what is being said, but I'm not sure that there is any clearer way for it to be put?

I continued with weekly emails to 'name and shame' those that were still in debt, until Omer came to the rescue with an ingenious idea.

"Bit of advice Brad, why don't you introduce the 'No Pay, No Play' rule. Everyone will pay up then!"

I could see the logic behind it but I honestly didn't fancy starting the season with only six players. My management skills had improved significantly in the last year, but even I am not that good. It was pretty clear though as to how Omer had made it as a

Managing Director. With such strict rules like that I bet he sacks his staff on a daily basis.

Amongst these emails that had been going back and forth, there had been discussions regarding a potential pre-season tour – not for this year but for July/August 2011. My initial research had been disappointing to say the least, until I stumbled across a company that wanted to arrange for us to go to Argentina for the week. It sounded amazing, until I was quoted in excess of two thousand pounds per player – I quickly deleted the email and, to this day, still have not replied to the regular 'chasers' that I receive from them.

With techniques and ways that I will not bore you with, I managed to get in contact with the physiotherapist for Limerick Football Club over in Ireland. Although nothing is yet confirmed (or paid for and you know how much fun I am going to have with that part) the discussed itinerary will see us come up against Limerick Under 20's on a Friday night and the Limerick Reserve Team on the Sunday afternoon. Not only are these a professional side that were scheduled to play a full strength Barcelona team in August (it sadly fell through due to complications with the Irish FA) but, by the time we arrive, will be slap-bang in the middle of their domestic season, potentially only two weeks away from their equivalent of the FA Cup Final. Amongst others, their squad consists of ex-Arsenal youngsters and we would be playing in their 4,000-seater stadium. Still, it's not Hanwell Town though is it?!

As I am writing this, the fixtures have been released for the new season. There will only be eight teams in our league this year, following promotions for The Masons Arms and Chefchaeoun Berbers. We will also be reunited with AFC Millbank who finished bottom of the Premier Division. On paper, the league title should be between Barnet Eagles, Millbank and ourselves but no team can be written off in this league.

I am expecting confidence to be high amongst the players with everybody now 'gelled' together as a unit. We have managed to keep the changes to a minimum as well, with the only loss being Shogo Hirata who has had to move to Swansea for a year with work. Captain Matty has reduced his availability on the grounds of 'family expansion' so we wish both him and Mrs Russell well – please let him come out to play now and again though! James Sharp has returned from his travels and rejoins up with the squad, as does a new face in Dan Mullins who is more than capable of carrying on where Matty left off.

With Pete Sharp being given the responsibility of the captain's armband and the experienced heads of Neil and Omer still in place there is absolutely no reason why this team cannot make the step up to the next level. We must remember though that this is Sunday League football and this is Nice Fridge Locomotiv and things do not always go as planned.

Football is a funny old game and anything can happen. However, there is one certainty – no matter the opposition, the conditions or the location, our squad of once-strangers will be there together, fully committed and wearing the famous Nice Fridge colours, with one common interest...

The Love Of The Game